THE WAY IT WAS

and

NOW

by

ROLY ARMITAGE, DVM, VS

Title: THE WAY IT WAS AND NOW

by: ROLY ARMITAGE, DVM, VS

ISBN-13: 978-1500996734

ISBN-10: 1500996734

Published by Roly Armitage

Cover, layout and editing by Mary Montague, m3m@rogers.com

TABLE OF CONTENTS

"Nothing is ever really lost to us as long as we remember it."

- *L.M. Montgomery, The Story Girl*

DEDICATION

This book is dedicated

to

my first wife

Mary

who was the mother of my four wonderful children
and who supported me in every aspect of my life,
making it possible for me to pursue my dreams

and

to

my second wife

Karen

who was my caring partner for the twenty years
that we had together.

Many hands make light work.

A Sincere Thank You

I would like to acknowledge the many people who, knowing of the wide and varied activities in which I have participated, have said, "Roly, you should write a book."

I specifically want to thank Mary Watson Montague; without her encouragement, direction, and active participation before and during its production, this book would never have come to fruition.

Also deserving of my special thanks is Anita Rutledge who spent many hours editing my manuscript.

A mother holds her children's hands
for a while...their hearts forever.
- Author Unknown

INTRODUCTION

As a young child I was very curious about what was contained in the secret pantry under the stairway that my mother always kept securely locked. It must be a great treasure I reasoned and, in fact, as I found out when she believed that her family of eight was mature enough to share its contents, it really was. Securely wrapped in tissue paper or packed in boxes were mementoes of her past and the generations that came before her - of a time in a distant country, a time of gentility and culture and of loved ones long passed. She, in her wisdom, realized that her heritage was a treasure to be cherished and passed down to her children so that they, in turn, would have a greater understanding of who came before them and who they were.

Each one of us has a secret store of memories of our past and I believe that it is now time for me to share mine.

If you have a spare minute, sit down
A spare three minutes, lie down
And you will live a healthy and happy life.
            My father, Godfrey Armitage

CHAPTER 1 - MY PARENTS

My mother's background was very privileged. Her mother had previously been married to Lord Sir Edward Drummond-Hay and she was Lady Alice Drummond-Hay. They were governor and governess of St. Helena's Island, a British possession where Napoleon had been exiled. During his term of office for the British government, Sir Edward was credited with the abolition of slavery on the island. He died while serving as governor and Lady Alice returned to England.

Eventually she met and married a young naval officer named John Foot and from that marriage they had two children, a boy and a girl. The daughter was my mother Joan Foot who was raised in a very precise way and controlled in her manner and etiquette.

When the first World War broke out in 1914 my father was about 36 years old and he enlisted immediately. He had trained in the reserves about two years before, so he was soon sent overseas. He was in the second battle of Ypres in Belgium. One day he survived a German mustard gas attack and on that very same day he was riding horseback on a single horse, drawing ammunition to the guns at the front when a shell hit nearby. His horse was hit and fell back on him. He was critically wounded and was shipped back to England, to St. George's Hospital.

Following her formal education and the outbreak of war in 1912, my mother volunteered as a Red Cross nurse and was appointed to duty at St. George's Hospital in London. Many of her patients were Canadian and British soldiers who had been wounded in France and Belgium. One of those patients was my father. While my mother nursed my father back to health they fell in love and soon married.

Father and Mother at the time of their wedding.

I recall my mother talking about my dad meeting her mother at their home which was situated near a small river. Since my father came from an area known as Constance Creek he asked my grandmother what was the name of the creek outside her place. My grandmother responded in her broad English accent, "Oh my dear, this is the mighty Thames."

My dad was a big man standing some six feet, six inches and weighed 250 pounds. After he joined the Army in Canada they had no uniform big enough to accommodate him, and he was sent overseas wearing ordinary trousers and a red sweater, with no hat because his hat size was 8½ and there was none available to fit him. The Army, however, did find a military tailor who made a uniform to fit him. My father was a buck private, or more properly called a gunner, which was the same level in the artillery, while my mother's brother was a colonel in the infantry which had just been evacuated from Dunkirk, and most of her relatives were high-ranking officers in the Army and Navy. For these reasons my mother's and father's marriage was not held in high esteem. However, after my mother had come to Canada, raised a large family and was obviously happy and successful, she was accepted by her family as having done the right thing.

All my brothers and sisters and myself know that we had the best parents in the world. We remember my mother telling us many stories of England and her childhood and upbringing. We lived through the depression years being humble but good citizens with little money available for unnecessary things. I remember that on my grandmother's death my mother received a substantial amount of money which, in 1938, allowed us to have electricity and full bathroom facilities established in our old but comfortable home.

The farm house where we were all raised.

I recall my mother's cousin who came from England for a visit. At that time or shortly thereafter, in 1939, we bought a brand-new Chevrolet sedan which was delivered to Carp in a crate and the cost was $800. In that same year, with my brother Robin as the driver, assisted by brave brother Bill, they took my mother and her cousin to the World's Fair in New York.

Deviating a bit, about my mother's background:

In 1936 she returned to England for a visit and also toured Germany. I remember when she returned she told us about all the children being organized by the Nazis in the Hitler regime, and she was very alarmed. Incidentally, this child training in Germany produced the same Hitler youth that was part of the 12th Panzer division who we faced in

Normandy in 1944, as I will discuss later in this book. Having been in Normandy myself, I witnessed their obviously well-trained troops.

I might mention that my mother's brother, my uncle, Patten Foot, was a colonel and commanding officer of Catterick Camp training center in Yorkshire, England. Shortly after I arrived in England in 1943 I went by bus from London to meet him. I arrived at the gate and was immediately paraded, meaning one soldier on each side of me all the way from the gate to my uncle's office. I was paraded into the building, still with the soldiers on each side, who were immediately dismissed by my uncle and the office door was closed. I can still see him sitting behind the desk with his mustache curled up on both ends, which was a typical style of distinction in the military.

I introduced myself and I can recall him saying in a very broad English accent, "Oh, you are Joan's son." It was rather a cold reception but was a typical military reception. However, when I met him at his residence later on I was treated with absolute love and affection, as the distance between my mother and him had improved over the years, socially that is. I later gave his name Patton to our second son, Blake Patton.

My mother lived to be 74, and my dad 85.

CHAPTER 2 - EARLY LIFE

My oldest brother, Maxwell James, was born in 1917. My mother came to Canada with him in her arms in late 1917, ahead of my father who was still in the Army but not in action. She stayed with my dad's sister in Ottawa until his arrival a year later. They

Mother with Maxwell James in Ottawa

resided at the original homestead on the Ottawa River in Dunrobin, Ontario. In 1923 my father purchased a 100-acre farm through the Veterans Land Act. I recall my neighbour saying that she saw my parents arrive at the new farm with my brother Bill in my mother's arms, and Robin was in the back of the horse-drawn buggy with the ducks.

Shortly after my father bought the farm a man came walking along the road. His name was Harry English; he was hungry and looking for work. My father and mother gave him a good meal and he did a small job as payment. As it turned out this man never left our farm and died there in 1946. He was an absolute gentleman who was a great help to my mother. Every one of the family loved him; he was a very independent individual but always had time to rub our heads if we, as children, had a problem. He is buried in our family plot at St. John's Anglican Church.

My first recollection as a young boy was when I had my fourth birthday. At that time my parents lived on a farm in South March, Ontario, and our neighbour, a very kind lady, invited me to come over to her home across the way in recognition of my birthday. My mother escorted me across the road and I was treated to a lovely cake and a small gift. The date was February 8, 1929, and it had to be the coldest day that year. My neighbour brought me back home and my mother met me halfway up the lane. I remember crying because of the cold and my mother tucking me under her skirt as we made our way back to our house.

I was the fourth boy in a family of eight, the fifth being a boy, the sixth and seventh were girls and the final child was a son.

I started to school at SS Number Two School and the teacher was Miss O'Keefe. As I recall, she was as kind as my mother. The school was a one-room school with eight rows of desks - the right-hand side was for grade one and the left-hand row was grade eight.

Peggy, Maxwell with June above, Robin, Bill, Roly, and Frank

My *crawl* from grade one to grade eight was rather uneventful but when I got into grade eight the teacher at that time was a man who had a bicycle for sale. I bought the bicycle with money from the sale of a calf that I had raised as my own. From that point on I spent more time on the bicycle and less time at school. It seemed that the teacher couldn't have cared less as to whether I was there or not, and consequently I failed and had to repeat the grade. The new teacher was Miss Reed and, because I was repeating, I was given my grade eight certificate and allowed to leave in April to work on the farm.

When I was in grade six and 12 years of age I was given the job of caretaker and one of my first jobs was to wash the schoolhouse floor. I knew this called for water to be used so I threw pail after pail of water on the floor. Before I finished mopping I went home for the day intending to finish the job the next morning. However when I came back the next day the floor had become a skating rink as the temperature was well below zero. With the help of people more learned than myself we got the fires burning and dried things up. I must add that the trustees of the school decided I was an unworthy candidate for the job until I was 16.

As part of a large family I did my share of farm work along with my brothers and sisters. The farm consisted of 100 acres and we had an average of about 20 milk cows, and six horses as most of the heavy work on the farm at that time was done with horses - although we eventually purchased a *Titan* tractor.

One of the advantages of having many siblings is that when combined with neighbour kids there was always enough players to make up a team. As soon as it was cold enough we would find an ice surface for a pick-up game of hockey. In that sport I participated from the time I was 12 and until the last time I put on skates to play competitively with the West Carleton Old-timers, at the age of 63. We played in Fort Lauderdale in a Can-Am Series – where in the last game I scored two goals. Speaking of scoring goals, long before that while playing in Amsterdam with the Canadian Army in an inter-regimental game we, the Artillery team, were playing the Signals team who incidentally had the All-Star Toronto Maple Leaf goalkeeper named Turk Broda in the nets. I scored on him and he autographed my puck. That is one of my treasured trophies.

• • •

My oldest brother joined the Air Force in 1938 and was one of the first people in the Ottawa area to lose his life in World War II. He was 23 years of age and was the brother born in England in 1917.

My next brother, Robin stayed on the farm during the war years. He had taken some military training one summer in the reserve army and was contemplating going on active duty when my dad asked him to stay on the farm because my brother Bill had joined the Navy and I had joined the Army. While he did this rather reluctantly, he nevertheless understood the situation and supported my mother's and dad's wishes. Robin married Lu Stanton, a resident of Fitzroy Harbour, but they had no children. Robin worked in the stationary engineering field along with his farming duties, while Lu worked in law firms at executive levels. Both Robin and Lu lived into their eighties and are now dead.

Brother Bill, now 91, spent the war years on a Corvette doing convoy duty on the Atlantic supporting convoys from Halifax to Great Britain and, incidentally, his Corvette along with another ship, was credited with the destruction of a

German submarine. Bill met and married a young lady from Northern Ireland named Shirley McWaters and they raised three girls, the eldest was Jillian and the youngest are twins, Elizabeth and Natalie.

Frank

I was next in line in the family and well mentioned in this book, so we now move on to my next brother Frank, who also joined the Canadian Army and served in several locations in Canada, but the war ended before he had the opportunity to go overseas. He worked his whole post-army life in the construction business at an executive level and died relatively young as the result of a brain tumor. Frank married Catherine Bradley from Stittsville, Ontario and they had five children, the eldest, Montie, short for Montgomery, was followed by Lynn, Laurie, Jeffery, and the youngest, a daughter Kelly.

The next member in our family was Peggy, a nickname; actually her real name was Veronica Margaret Joan. Following high school and during the war years she worked with the Taxation Department in Ottawa. Peggy eventually married George Scott; a chartered accountant and they had two boys, Gregory and Kingsley. Peggy died relatively young as the result of the big *C,* a very common and dreaded disease.

Next in line was June who worked for the federal government and married a young architect named Brian Pye. They had four children, the eldest Joanne was followed by their only son Robin, and then Nancy and the youngest, Barbara.

Kingsley

The youngest of my eight living siblings is Kingsley, born in 1931. Following high school he joined the Royal Canadian Mounted Police. He married Heather McAllister and they raised four children, the eldest, Blair, was followed by Neil, then their only daughter Fay, and the youngest son, Jim.

Sadly, my mom and dad lost two baby boys, born separately between my two eldest brothers Maxwell and Robin.

Robin, Bill, Roly, Frank, Peggy, June, and Kingsley

CHAPTER 3 - JOINING UP AND OVERSEAS

In 1941 when I was a student at Ottawa Technical high school I joined the Governor General's Foot Guards which was a twice-a-week sort of thing, and I remained a member of that organization for a year until 1942 when I was 17.

I was in grade ten in Ottawa when one day Eddie Nash and I went for a walk at noon hour. We went down Albert Street and saw a long lineup at one of the main buildings. There were two people in the lineup who we knew, George Blair and Earl Gow.

We went up to them and asked, "What are you doing?

"We're joining the Army," was the reply.

In fact they were both people who were what they called *categoried*, which meant that there was no way the Army would accept them. By going through the process of joining up they would get a document that said they weren't fit for military service and they would not be called up if there was a conscription later on.

I said to Eddie, "Why don't we get in line."

We did and we were in the Army by three o'clock in the afternoon.

An amusing thing is worth mentioning. The medical consisted of them using a stethoscope to check our lungs and heart, and then we were asked how old we were and a couple of other questions. I said I was eighteen and was asked for my birth certificate. I responded that I hadn't brought it with me but I could get it. The examiner said "You don't need it right now. You will be getting four days leave after you get accepted, and if you are you can bring it in then." So after receiving our uniforms we were transferred over to the Central Canada Exhibition building at the south part of Lansdowne Park. Underneath this building was the sleeping area for the recruits. Since my friend Eddie was behind me all the way, I said to him, "My new military number is C100222 , yours must be 223." "No," he said, "mine's 227." I said, "How come, Eddie, you were behind me all the way through?" And he replied, "You know that little bottle and the urine sample, well I went into the washroom and I just couldn't get things to work, so by the time I got out, four other people had gotten between us."

We were in the Army and about the same time we were expected home. I called and told my mother about what had happened. Since she was a First World War bride and my father having served in the artillery in that war, they were militarily oriented. Furthermore, as I mentioned earlier, my oldest brother had already been killed in the Royal Canadian

Air Force in July of 1940 - the first local casualty in the Ottawa area.

We did our training in Ottawa, and I remember that my father said to me in a jovial manner, "Make sure you join the artillery and you won't have to walk like in the infantry."

I did take his advice; this was April, 1942 and I was sent to Petawawa, Ontario, for a month's training. We were just starting to train on artillery pieces when a bulletin came around that the the first Canadian Paratroop battalion was being formed. I thought it would be interesting, so I made an application. The recruiting officer asked me if I realized the hazards of this type of deployment and I said, "Yes and I am ready to accept whatever comes."

Following my interview with the recruiter for the paratroopers I had a very extensive medical which included listening to my lungs, checking my heart, doing exercises and running. Finally I was notified that I had been accepted for training.

We assembled back at the exhibition grounds in Ottawa in Lansdowne Park. There were some 350 recruits and we were informed that we would be going to Georgia in the USA for training.

We arrived in Georgia by train, and after some two weeks, 30 of the recruits where called out by name and the American officer said, "Now hear this all of you who are 18 years of age - the United States government has established a new rule that says all foreign troops must be 19 years of age or more to train on our soil."

As a consequence, we were sent back to Ottawa by train and dispersed to our original units which, in my case, was the Artillery in Petawawa. Upon my arrival I noticed that there was a need for dispatch riders in the Army and a training course was to be held in Woodstock, Ontario. The course was for two months. I took that course between August and October, 1942, which involved taking a motorcycle apart and putting it back together again, and training for a full month and ending with making airborne jumps off ramps.

Upon graduation I returned to Petawawa and became a dispatch rider. One of my first duties was to deliver mail to a prisoner-of-war camp at a nearby fenced-in facility. I believe the name was Clear Lake. Some days later an officer stopped me and asked if I was eligible for overseas duty. I said yes, and I was immediately sent on embarkation leave, and some ten days later I was on a train to Halifax.

The trip was uneventful with only one stop in New Brunswick for exercise in a field with some 500 recruits. The fence around the exercise area was well guarded to prevent the escape of anyone with a personal change of heart about going overseas.

We arrived at Halifax where the ocean liner, the Queen Elizabeth was waiting. Going up the gangplank was a line of RCMP officers to make sure we made the trip from the train to the ship. We had name tags on our chests which were removed as we entered the ship to prove that we had gone aboard.

The Queen Elizabeth painted in wartime grey

The ship was made to carry 2000 passengers - I repeat 2000 passengers, but this day there were 22,000 troops onboard. Each individual cabin had 21 beds which were hammocks in seven rows of three deep. After I was assigned to a specific cabin and hammock I slid into it like going into a tube. When I looked left, the other man on the same level was Russ McKay, a bomber pilot in the Royal Canadian Air Force, going overseas for duty. All I can say at this point is that it was quite a coincidence that we were so close together for the trip from Halifax to Scotland because out of the 22,000 on board he was the only one I knew because he was from Carp, Ontario and had been a good friend of my brother's. We arrived in Scotland after three days and eight hours which was a record crossing for the ship. The speed was necessary in case of enemy submarines.

Since the boat was so laden with the weight of people it was deep in the water and could not go up the Clyde River into the dock at the port Greenock, hence we were taken ashore by tender[1], and I remember Boy Scouts helping us with our baggage.

We went by train to southern England to our first military camp in Surrey. Since I arrived as a dispatch rider we commenced training in a large pit known as the Devil's Punch Bowl. One day going up a hill at about a 45° angle I was losing speed as I neared the top, so I leaned backwards on the back wheel of my motorcycle, and it went airborne. I ended up in the hospital for three weeks - nothing dangerous, just cuts and bruises. I was told after that I was not suitable as a dispatch rider because of my *carriage physique*; I was considered top-heavy.

This reminds me that when I was born my mother said I was square in physique, whereas most of my brothers had been long and thin at birth. When my father saw me for the

---

1 *on smaller boats*

first time he said to my mother, "What's that?" She said, "This is my roly-poly." Hence my father gave me the name Roly.

When I had been examined for the paratroopers it was found that I had excellent night vision so the Army assigned me to be an observer in the artillery. About then we went for five-month's training in England going all the way from the south of England to the Cheviot Hills at the north, just south of the Scottish border.

CHAPTER 4 - WARTIME EXPERIENCES

My dad's advice was to join the artillery so I would not have to walk, but I can assure you that we did do a lot of walking between the South of England to just south of Scotland where the only living thing was the odd sheep. This was the first time in our five-month training that we used live ammunition and we really tried not to interfere with normal farm work. Actually this training was the culmination of a lot of work we had done over the last year in preparing for our many positions in future battles. For example: gunners, observers, plotters and range finders and, of course, the infantry regiments were doing the same, to be ready when the big day came. We all knew that someday we would be going into combat to alleviate the terrible conditions that existed in Europe.

We returned from Scotland to Coulsdon in Surrey and I recall seeing a *Doodle Bug* V2, which was a live bomb that was one of hundreds sent from Germany to England with just sufficient fuel to make its way to London. The very first one we saw was coming over at about 1000 feet with a Spitfire beside it. The Spitfire very dramatically with its own wing tipped the wing of the flying V2 bomb and sent it crashing downward. It crashed about a mile from where we were in a farmer's barnyard. We ran the distance to see what damage had been done and when we looked around the farm yard it was completely devastated - there were several chickens and the odd animal running around, and some were dead. As I looked around I saw an egg in a nest still quite warm and I picked it up - the first real egg I had seen for some time. Just then over my shoulder I saw who was obviously the owner of the farm and he said in a very broad English accent, "Okay Canada, don't take the only fucking thing that is left." But then he said, "On second thought, you Canadians are doing a lot for us so you can have the egg." Eventually, back at the barracks I cooked and enjoyed it.

After that we were informed that we were moving to the coast of England obviously in preparation for things that were going to happen there. There were large concentrations of troops in the southern English area, notably close to the dry docks. The announcement came that the tremendous D-Day Armada had commenced on the morning of June 6th, 1944.

We, the heavier 100-pound shell artillery, would not be going on the first landing in France, but the 25-pounders of the 3rd Division were part of the initial wave, and on that very day I developed mumps and had to go to hospital. However, I didn't miss anything because our regiment was not designated to go at that time anyway. So actually on 18th of June we were loaded and transported onto the large *USS George Whyte* liberty class ship at the Londonderry Docks in London on the Thames River. It took almost 24 hours to load the boat. Then one evening we slipped out, passed the White Cliffs of Dover into the English Channel and serenely drifted during the night. In the morning we could see the coast of France.

My first recollection is of a lot of fires on the coast. We anchored about one mile off the coast and prepared for disembarking. Right beside us was Her Majesty's Royal Navy Battleship, the *Rodney* with its four barrels sending salvos - firing constantly because, as I said, there was no heavy artillery there yet and they were supporting the infantry, obviously by radio signal. The noise was almost unbelievable! The only fear I had really, as we were in the hold at the bottom of the ship, so crowded and smelly, was the thought of being hit with a German submarine, so I sneaked up on deck. I wasn't there long until my officer spotted me and ordered me to go back down.

In any case, a landing barge came beside our ship with large winches and cranes to unload the guns and vehicles. Running the barge were two English *Tommys*[2] who were running the large equipment lifting our guns and trucks, and other materials, down onto the landing craft. Suddenly everything stopped, and when our officer inquired as to what the problem was one of the Tommys replied, "It's ten o'clock SIR and we're just stopping to have a spot of tea." And sure enough, they had some water heating and were in the

---

2 *Slang for an English soldier.*

process of preparing it. Our officer went and swiped all the tea-making paraphernalia overboard with the order, "Get back to work." That was my first exposure to the 'work-to-rule' concept, because things had slowed to a snail's pace for a time.

We went down over the edge on a net draped over the side of the boat onto the landing craft and we went ashore. The landing craft didn't quite make it to the shore so we had to bail out but all the vehicles, which had been waterproofed, drove into deep water and made it safely. Somehow or other I ended up getting wet, and I don't remember or understand how that happened for I should have been in the vehicle.

Nevertheless, as I recall, I was a bit nervous and wanted to get ashore as soon as possible. I didn't dry out for two weeks. I might add that there were hundreds of German prisoners on the beach as we landed, and they were loaded onto the barges and taken out to the ships for transport back to England to be housed. That was the end of the war for them, but we were just getting initiated.

It is my intent, in this ongoing dialogue regarding the war itself, to stay away from actual action memories and talk more about the ways and the places we fought, as a lot of the fighting would not make good reading.

The first engagement we had with the enemy was at Carpiquet Airport because the military needed the airport badly for aircraft to land and for repeated sorties. At the same time they had laid a steel net all the way along the shore for Typhoons and Mustangs and other fighter aircraft, to land, reload their machine guns and take off. It took us three days under continual shelling between our 3rd Medium Artillery[3] and German artillery to get the airport into Canadian hands.

It was thought initially that the Army would be in the city of Caen within 24 hours of landing on June 6th, but it took a whole month to get there, which indicates the type of fighting and resistance that was in front of us as we fought our way through wheat fields and open country to Caen. We were facing the German 12th Panzer Division and paratroops mostly made up of fanatical Hitler youth who were hardened and fierce. Then eventually we found ways, with the Canadians on the left and Americans on the right, where we had almost encircled the German army in front of us. However, there was this one small part of the circle that had not yet been closed. It was called the Falaise Gap. This gap was a distance of about two miles long and existed as an escape route for the Germans from the encircled area into open country. This route underwent constant strafing by our allied aircraft and allied artillery. The result was thousands of dead German soldiers, Belgian horses along with disabled trucks, artillery pieces and other German army equipment spread along the escape route. This whole mess took 12

---

3 *3rd Medium Regt. Royal Canadian Artillery meaning we had medium sized shells.*

hours to clear with four D-8 bulldozers of the Royal Canadian Engineers. As we passed through following the clean-up, the smell was unbearable to the point where we had to wear our gas masks. Many of the enemy escaped before the gap was closed, but nevertheless several thousand Germans were captured at Falaise. Two weeks later on July 29th, under heavy shelling, my own officer, Lieut. Roy Pattinson, was killed.

Two or three days after my officer's death we were told to *dig in* as we were going to be there for awhile so I dug my slit trench, or so called foxhole, to be under cover from expected German shelling. I remembered seeing a piece of tarpaulin on the side of the road and I went down to get it for the top of my foxhole to make it more *deluxe* and rainproof. On the way back the Germans started shelling heavily and I dropped the tarp and ran for my slit trench. When I got there two other men were in my trench and I jumped in on top of them. I was pretty close to the surface and when a shell hit 30 feet away the blast blew me out of the hole. I received severe concussion damage. I might add I do not remember any part of this happening, so obviously a person could be killed and have no pain or suffering.

When I was at the first aid post where I was taken by our medics I eventually realized where I was. They were going to send me back to England but I said I felt pretty good and didn't deserve that - that I would be okay eventually. As a result of the blast I suffered permanent loss of hearing in my left ear and my right ear was also damaged.

In a few days all the bells stopped ringing and my headaches went away. I helped the medical officer and medics for a few days with incoming patients but soon was back to my normal duties. To this day I wear a hearing aid and, even with it, my hearing is not even close to normal.

Nothing else happened to me while we travelled the route along the coast. We were involved in the liberation of Calais and Boulogne and moved north into Belgium. Our first encounter with any real resistance was in the Bruges Brussels area, and following that we moved towards Antwerp.

Antwerp was necessary as a port because up until this point all supplies of food and ammunition had to be brought up from the beachhead at Courseulles-sur-Mer, better known as Juno Beach, where we originally landed. Actually at this point the allies had built an artificial harbour called Mulberry Dock; with this system the ships would pull up to the end and the trucks would bring the supplies ashore. A channel port was really necessary and so the battle for the clearance of the Scheldt Estuary commenced and, without going into too many details, the port of Antwerp was freed and paid-for dearly with many killed and injured clearing the numerous Walcheren Islands where the German fortifications were immense.

Then on to Bergen op Zoom in the Netherlands where many Canadians lie buried in the cemetery there. At this point the military services needed an airport again and we moved across the top of Belgium to Eindhoven and took the airport there to be used by the Allies. We then moved north to Nijmegen in the Arnhem area, and the city of Arnhem being known principally for the film 'The Bridge Too Far.'

Soon after getting a brief rest away from it all, the Germans attacked the Americans who were defending the port of Antwerp, which had just a month before been put into operations for delivery of supplies. This was a surprise attack and the Americans were caught off-guard so to speak; the fighting that ensued became known as *The Battle of the Bulge.*

We went back down in a hurry and helped put a stop to the attack, shelling constantly for two days. The Germans captured a lot of supplies from the Americans which both sides needed badly.

After this very successful operation we returned to Nijmegen and we stayed there from late November and December and into January 1945. It was now winter with a lot of snow and a lot of dirty weather. I recall a very happy Christmas with all the trimmings, served by our officers to the other ranks. About twenty of us, slept in the fire hall and our gunners sent the odd gun-fire over into Germany just to let them know we were still around, and they, in turn, did likewise.

In early January of 1945 and for days thereafter we spent a lot of lot of time planning our move into Germany which was about twenty miles away. On my birthday, February 8, 1945, every gun in the Canadian Army fired at midnight and we moved into Germany through the night, through the Reichswald forest and Hochwald forest into open country, and before morning we had flattened the town of Kleve. Then we turned north and crossed the Rhein River at Emmerich on the pontoon bridges built by Canadian engineers. We moved north through Oldenburg, Germany and then back into Holland to liberate the area of Apeldoorn where one of the Dutch Queen's residences was located. We stayed there for two to three days, in the palace as *residents*. Then we left and went back to Germany. We moved north to Wilhelmshaven where the German submarine base was situated.

On May 5, 1945, the war came to an end. I don't know how to explain how we all felt about this moment - that finally it was all over and that we had survived. I recall an amusing letter I had received from my uncle who told me to hide behind every tree possible to survive because he was going to give me his farm when I returned. So obviously I had followed his instructions.

A rather amusing thing happened about that time. We were going so fast we outstripped the kitchen and when we put our thoughts together we were at a church that we were going to use as an observation post. We often did that because when we climbed up into the belfry it was possible to see for miles around. I recall my officer realizing that we were a little hungry and we should think about finding out where the kitchen was. I said to Captain King that about a mile back I had seen three of four chickens in a pen behind a house. I said let me go back and I will get one of them. As I came from a farm I was pretty good at killing a chicken. So I went back with the Jeep and one other person. I crawled in under the fence and as I was catching the chicken, a lady came to the door. If eyes could kill I would be dead.

She had her hands on her hips and she was looking at me catching the chicken. Nevertheless I got out under the wire and drove back to the church with the chicken. I had already wrung its neck and with the bayonet from my rifle, skinned the bird and withdrew the innards. There was a little creek going by so we quartered the chicken and thoroughly washed it in the creek and then, finally, the question was, "What are we going to cook this in?" One of the boys, I remember his name was Dubeau, a French-speaking man from Montreal, said in his broken English, "Excusay-moi, for me dare, I tink I have an idea." He went into the church and brought out the brass lining of the font that babies are christened in. He took it down to the creek and scoured it with sand and brought it up full of water, then we poured a little gasoline on the ground and with three or four stones to support the font we eventually had a very good feed of chicken. He then took the pot down to the creek and cleaned it up the best he could then put it back in the church. I am sure that to this day German children are being christened in a pot that was used to cook chicken.

Since the war was now over we went back to Holland and all gathered together at the city of Utrecht, which is the seat of the veterinary college in Holland, and we stayed in that building for three or four days.

Eventually we had to make a decision of three things that were offered us. First go home right now and get 30 days' leave and return to join the army of occupation. Or, we could go home right now, get 30 days' leave and go to take part in the Japanese war which was still going on. Third, the first to come overseas would be the first to go home for good; in other words you went back according to the date you arrived overseas from Canada, and I was told that I would be going home in January 1946, and this was May 1945.

I elected to go home right now because I thought if I signed up to go to Japan that somehow or other I would get out of the Army when I got home. One of my officers came to me and said, "Roly, what did you do?" I told him I'd signed to go to Japan and was sure my influential father would get me out to work on our home farm. He said that he understood my thinking, but before the war he had had some hotel experience and the Canadian Army was opening a leave centre in a large hotel up on the North Sea in Noordwijk aan Zee in Holland. It was called Huis ter Duin and he said that he was going to be in charge and he'd like me to come to work with him and look after the operations end of things. It didn't take long for me to make up my mind. I hand-picked about 30 soldiers from my regiment to work on the staff to help with the operation of the hotel.

When we arrived at the hotel, its furniture was spread out in different places in the country and we had to bring it back to the hotel. Also on the beach in front of the hotel was a large cement wall extending all the way down for miles, covered with barbed wire as a sort of defence against landing at that area. This had to be removed so while we were there we cut a large hole in the wall to allow us to get to the beach to sweep the area for mines. Later the army engineers dug a trench beside the wall and tipped it into the excavation, covered it with the sand on the beach, and that is where the wall is to this day.

After we got the hotel up and running, soldiers would come to the hotel and stay for three days and then be replaced by the next bus load of beach and holiday seekers from the regiment. We had an orchestra and girls would come from the surrounding towns of Leiden, Noorwijk, and others by army bus to the dances.

We also had the use of a second hotel for any overflow of guests. This was the Noordzee *(North Sea)* Hotel, owned and managed by Nicolaas van Beelen. He was a bachelor at the time but later married and had a son called Hans, and two daughters, Geertrui and Anneke, both of whom have visited me here in Canada. Geertrui actually lives in Invermere, B.C., Canada while Anneke is a veterinarian in Holland.

We guaranteed their parents that they would be well chaperoned while there and would be taken back home by bus. That went on for the whole summer without any problems or incidents.

To digress a little. When we were in Germany and the war was in full gear, my friend and I were at a large farm which had been vacated. There was nobody there but there was a 1932 Chevrolet staff car in the yard, camouflaged in colour but in beautiful condition. My friend said, "You know what Roly, l would like to hide this car and maybe someday come back and get it." I replied, "How are you going to do that?" Eventually we took the car over behind the barn and covered it with hay from a nearby stack Then we marked down the map references of the farm on a piece of paper.

One day at the hotel we decided to go back to see if we could find the car. I had a Jeep and when we went there the car was still in the same place and the farm house was still vacant. We put gas in the tank and he followed me back to the hotel where we parked the car in the hotel garage.

In those days I had to travel to Rotterdam to get kegs of beer and to Amsterdam to get various liquors. One day a young man came up to me on a bicycle and asked if he could buy some petrol. I informed him that it was a standing military rule that there was to be no sale of petrol to anyone. He then said he understood, but asked if it would be possible to trade beer for petrol as his family had a large brewery in Holland. I told him I did not have the last say and I said, "Follow me and I will introduce you to Captain King, and by the way, what is your name?" He said, "Freddie Heineken."

Obviously they made a deal because all summer we traded beer of which we used lots. I met him off and on during our stay at the hotel but didn't see him again much after that. At that time he was 22 years of age – two years older than I was. He also told me that he was going to go to the United States to study English and marketing at Harvard University – that was in 1946. While he was in the United States he apparently did a pretty good job because his company was selling as much beer there as they were in Holland.

Before he came back years later, he was put in charge of marketing in his family's brewery. I recall speaking to him once or twice later by telephone. He did tell me that his father had been selling a lot of the shares in the company, to the point where they did not have control anymore. Then his grandmother, his father's mother, said to Freddie, "Anytime you can buy shares do so, and I'll give you the money." Sometime later he told the chairman of the board that he was going to the United States and the chairman said, "Freddie, you will have to get permission from the board." Freddie replied, "Excuse me, but I now have 53% of the shares and I will talk about things when I get back."

I understand that Freddie was kidnapped in the late 1980s and was held in a dungeon for about three weeks where he contracted a fungal infection in his lungs. The company paid a ransom of some 35 million guilder, the highest ransom ever, and upon his release the ringleader of the kidnappers was captured. I understand some 20 million of the money was recovered, while the rest disappeared. I spoke with Freddie in 2002 when I was going back to Holland for a visit, and he said he was unable to receive me because he was too sick. He died that year. In 2002 I received a letter from his wife, Martha, thanking me for the memories of our association.

At the end of our five months at the hotel we were told we were going to England, so three weeks before our departure we took the car, which my friend had painted green, down to Brussels where there was a black market for cars. When we were there we did a little partying and one night my friend got a little bit out of control and caused enough disturbance that the bartender called the military police and they came and arrested him and another friend who was with us. He at least saved my hide by telling the police that I was not part of their group. Of course, I agreed with that and I went to the local army quarters to sleep.

The next morning I went to the local army detention centre and told the guard attendant that we had been informed that they were holding two of our regimental soldiers in confinement, and that I was here to pick them up and discipline them accordingly. He marched them out and, as I was a sergeant, I bellowed at them to stand at attention while I signed them out.

Obviously we were back in business and sold the car for a sum of 400 pounds, the pound then being worth $4.50 Canadian, so we had sufficient funds to have a bit of fun. Later, when we got back to the hotel in Noordwijk, we still had two weeks before we closed up the centre in late November 1945. Our regiment then went to England and settled into an army barracks in Croydon, London, where we would be waiting two weeks to take the Queen Elizabeth ship back to Canada from the port of Southampton.

I had a pocketful of money and decided to go to Ireland, as my father had asked me to try and visit if I could, to see where our forefathers had lived in Tipperary prior to their emigrating to Canada in 1826. I took a train to Liverpool and a bus to the port of departure on the channel and crossed by ferry to Dublin. I checked into a first-class hotel, had a large steak dinner and then went out and asked the first policeman I saw if there were any dances locally. I remember him saying in his broad Irish accent that there was one just around the corner. I found it and, *low and behold,* there was a Canadian Navy Wren Petty Officer there, also on a leave from Glasgow where she was stationed. We danced the night away, met the next morning for breakfast, and toured the town for three more days before she had to go back to Scotland, so I decided to cancel Ireland and go back with her. We were there for a few more days and then I took a train to Southampton and soon was going up the gangplank for the trip home. I didn't have enough money left for a hot dog. Obviously the past ten days had been memorable.

We sailed to New York and I recall seeing the Statue of Liberty and then slowly sailing into the city proper where we were greeted with horns from boats as we went by. I remember crossing a bridge on foot into New Jersey and the Salvation Army greeting us with hot coffee. We went to our designated trains going to different parts of Canada. My group was told to go to train three which was going to Ottawa. Somehow or other that was erroneous because the train went to Cornwall on its way to Toronto, so we were delayed in the Cornwall station as the Stormont and Glengarry Highlanders were disembarking and meeting their families. We went on with the train and got off at Brockville and waited for the train coming from Toronto to get us to Ottawa.

When we got on the train to Ottawa, one of our boys had gotten a little bit too much to drink while we were waiting, and we were not going to let him meet his family in that condition. So we asked the train man if he could detain this person for a couple of hours until he sobered up enough to meet his family, which he agreed to do. He said there was another train coming in two hours and he would hold the boy until that time.

We had a very joyous reunion in the station in Ottawa and I remember my dad saying to me, "Oh Roly, did you get to Ireland?" Of course, I had to tell him that I had changed my plans, and I told him the story about the girl in the Navy and going to Glasgow and he said with a laugh, "Roly, I'd have done the same."

While in the station I saw a couple looking for their soldier son, so I went over and asked if their name was Proulx. When they said it was I told them their son got delayed, and would be on the next train from Toronto in about two hours. They went back and had a seat again to wait for their soldier hero to arrive.

We went home that night to a tremendously happy homecoming. All the neighbours were at the farm in South March.

It was a joyous and memorable event to be home after three years.

CHAPTER 5 - ADAPTING TO CIVILIAN LIFE

After the celebration of my homecoming at the farm in early January 1946 the decision about where to go from there was urgent. I did not particularly want to work on the farm, and I recalled advice from my last officer, Lieut. Goldsmith, when we were bidding farewell to each other after the war. He had reached up and tapped me on the temple with his index finger and said, "Sgt., promise me that when you get home you will get yourself a formal education because you can handle it." Actually that was the first time in my life that anyone had told me I was half-intelligent.

I legally had 30 days leave with pay and a civilian clothing allowance after my discharge. I decided to inform the discharge officer that I wanted to go back to school. He looked at my papers and said, "My God, you only have grade nine; the best we have to offer is a program of accelerated education in Brockville, Ontario, leading to grades 12 and 13 graduation. Incidentally, there is a new course starting on the first of February." Without a moment of hesitation, I said to him, "Give me the papers and I'll report on Monday." I felt pretty confident that I could handle it as I had used trigonometry extensively during my duties finding line and range in the artillery.

I started a grade 12 class in February 1945 and took seven subjects that were necessary to get into veterinary college, which is where I had decided I wanted to go. The subjects were Algebra, Physics, Geometry, Chemistry, Botany, Zoology, English and History. We took two subjects at a time for a full month and then wrote them off, picked up two more and so on. We were in school from from eight o'clock in the morning until noon, and then from one in the afternoon until five o'clock, had dinner, and then two more hours in the evening, every day except Saturday which was eight in the morning until noon. The period from seven to nine in the evening was to ask questions and prepare for the next day. We had Sundays off.

At the end of June I had my Junior matriculation. In July I started under the same program and subjects and had my grade 13 by December 17. The failure rate was 50%.

The board of admittance to the University of Guelph Veterinary College sat in January 1947. I made my application using my present marks and was accepted, subject to an interview.

On the day of the interview I was waiting to go in to be heard when another man was standing close by for the same purpose. We introduced ourselves and both of us were accepted on interview. This man eventually became a very close friend.

The rest of the winter I spent with a cousin of mine cutting out a large basswood bush that my father and my cousin's father owned in common. We worked all winter and in the spring we received an offer from a lumber company in Ottawa for $40 a thousand board feet, subject to us delivering the logs to the mill. We got another offer for the same price but they said they would truck the logs in. We immediately accepted the last offer with the company which would truck the logs from the bush to the mill.

When the lumber had been prepared and measured we went in to get a cheque and were confronted with police who prevented us from entering saying that the mill had gone bankrupt and we would have to make a claim for our money. The *short* of the story is that the banks had preference to their assets and we were considered ordinary claimants. The *long* of the story is that we were paid 3.8 cents on the dollar, not even enough to pay for the rental of the horse that we had used in our endeavour. Our total loss was in the neighbourhood of $4000.00 or two thousand dollars each, and in the year 1947, $4000 was a lot of money. My $2000 had been earmarked to support my way through veterinary college.

Chapter 6 - Marriage and Family

Prior to my going overseas and shortly after I had joined the Army I attended a church play which was being performed in a hall in Dunrobin, Ontario. The play was being put on by the Stittsville United Church. The play was called *Mother-in-law Blues*. One of the star players in the play was a

Mary Spearman

young lady about 16 or 17 years old, who was playing the part of an airline stewardess. I was totally infatuated by her beauty and made a point of saying hello to her when the play was over. She very kindly gave me her telephone number and told me where she lived. Later on I made contact.

On three or four occasions we had dates and on returning each time to her house I was never invited in. I left it at that, until one day while we were driving through my hometown area I pointed out the church that we were passing as *my* Anglican Church. After we got to her home - it was on a weekend, around noon - she ran into the house. A short time later her mother appeared and invited me in for lunch. I remember distinctly her words, "Now Roly come in for dinner and meet the family." I wondered why I was finally being asked in but on a later date I was told by my girlfriend, Miss Mary Spearman, that her mother had learned from her that I was a Protestant and not a Catholic. Her mother had thought that because I came from an area which was predominantly Catholic that I was one and therefore not welcome in their Protestant home. There was really nothing wrong with this because it was definitely a common attitude of the times. Protestants and Catholics were considered to be non-compatible, two very different kinds of people, and parents did not want their children to marry outside of their faith.

Mary and I were eventually married on June 28, 1947 in the Stittsville United Church. Our first boy was born November 3, 1948 while I was in my first year of university at Guelph, and Mary was at home with her family. I desperately wanted to be present at the time of the birth but, of course, I was in the middle of my fall exams. I was totally delighted to receive the call that Maxwell Gordon was born. Let me deviate a bit here to say that the name 'Maxwell Gordon' was derived from the names of my first brother who was killed in 1940 while serving in the Air Force and Mary's brother Gordon who also died during the Second World War in Bomber Command on a mission over enemy territory.

Alas, there was no trace of his demise as they did not return from action and to this day there is no record of where they crashed.

Shortly after I graduated as a veterinarian we moved to Shawville, Quebec in 1951 and our daughter, Ann Elizabeth, was born there in 1953, followed by Blake Patton in 1954, and our final and last child, James Donald who was born in 1957. My wife, Mary, was actually a very small woman and I am a rather large individual physically, so our children weren't very small at birth and consequently all four were born by Cesarean section.

CHAPTER 7 - MY BEST FRIEND – BLAKE GRAHAM

I moved to Guelph in the fall of 1947 to commence my veterinary studies and my good friend whom I had met at the time of the interview, Blake Graham was his name, and I decided to room together at the college. Blake had completed high school over a five-year period and had recently graduated. He was absolutely brilliant. Since my courses in high school were abbreviated and not as English-oriented as was his, I can't tell you how much he helped me with my English, and how best to study.

The University was only in a position to graduate 100 veterinarians per year and had accepted 160 applicants. On the first day the professor said, "Look left and right, one in four of you will not be here in the spring." They dismissed 46 following the fall exams and another 14 in the spring, and they had their number, which was all the University could handle at any one time. Obviously I survived but I was 80th in standing, 20th from the bottom. The following year I stood 56th in my class, following the third-year I stood 31st. In the final and graduating year there were 19 students who received first-class honours and I was number 11.

During the time I was at the college I played football and hockey but only at an intramural level. The nurse in the first-aid building was someone who had been there for many years and I must say I have never met a more pleasant person. However, one day after receiving a minor injury I reported to the infirmary and, lo and behold, I was greeted by the most beautiful woman I'd seen for some time. She introduced herself as the new nurse. Following my treatment I immediately ran to my room and said to Blake, "You have to fake an injury and go to the nursing station!" which he did. The long and short of the story was that Blake and Barbara were married the day after we graduated on May 22, 1951 and I was best man at the wedding. From that day until July 2013 when Blake died he was my very best friend. I named my second son Blake in his honour, and now I have a great-grandson by the same name. Unfortunately my own son, Blake, died a rather tragic death on the farm at age 27.

My son, Blake, had been married to Mary Lou, a very beautiful and charming young lady, for only two years or so. Together they had built a lovely log home, cut from the bush by hand and built with many friends helping. Mary Lou was a teacher at a local high school at the time of Blake's death. Later, while teaching in Ottawa, Mary Lou met a very fine man called Dave Ellis, who also was a schoolteacher - actually a principal. They married and eventually had two children. One day Dave invited me to the log house to meet his mother. When I was introduced to Mrs. Ellis she said hello to me in a very distinct English accent.

Since my mother was English and I had served in England during the war I was very aware of the accent. I said, "Oh you must be from England." She agreed and I immediately told her that I had been overseas in England during the war and asked her where her home had been. She replied, "Oh it was a very small village in Surrey." I asked her to be more specific since I had been stationed in Surrey and was quite familiar with that area. She said that her home was in Coulsdon. I was absolutely shocked and told her, "Would you believe that's where I was stationed." She was surprised and said, "You were those soldiers in the large park?" "Yes," I said and added jokingly, "just a minute, Mrs. Ellis, let me get a closer look at that boy of yours." She immediately picked up the reference with a smile and said, "No, no, no, he was born in 1943 and you guys were there only in 1944." We laughed about that for the next few minutes. Humour at any time is fun.

CHAPTER 8 - MY VETERINARY CAREER

Between third and fourth years in veterinary college it was imperative that we spend two months with the Federal Government. One month in meat inspection, and one month in field work notably blood testing cattle and control of contagious diseases. I did my meat inspection at Canada Packers in Hull, Quebec as veterinary inspection in Canada is mandatory before and after slaughter. The other month I spent in the Shawville, Quebec area blood testing cattle for brucellosis.

While I was in Shawville many farmers asked where I was going to practice after graduation the next year. I told them I had not made up my mind but due to the fact that the resident veterinarian in Shawville wanted to retire I would consider dialoguing with him regarding my availability as a replacement.

I graduated from veterinary college in 1951 and after much consideration I decided to go to Shawville, subject to writing my Quebec exams. I moved there on June 1st, 1951 and rented a house on the main Street. And I might add here that I remained in Shawville until January 1st, 1970. My practice consisted mainly of cattle with limited small animal work. In addition I took on the work of looking after the approximately 1000 horses involved in lumber operations in western Quebec. Those large lumber operations used approximately 500 horses on the go at all times. I contracted a local aircraft to fly into the various locations at specific intervals to care for the general welfare of the horses and also to handle emergencies.

About that time I also looked after several racehorses in the Shawville area and gained a special and sincere interest in horse racing, to the point that not much later I purchased my first racing horse. That went on to be a lifelong hobby.

In 1954 I also took on the duties of track veterinarian at Connaught Park Raceway at Aylmer, Quebec and this brings to mind a rather interesting story. One of my clients at the track was a man named Paddy Mitchell who owned a total of three or four horses. I treated one for a problem at about 9:30 in the morning with Paddy in attendance. Within 24 hours it was announced on the news that there had been a very large gold heist at the Ottawa Airport. The announcement went on to inform us that Paddy and an accomplice had been accused of the crime. That was on the very same day that at 12 noon I had treated his horse. Shortly thereafter they were both apprehended and sent to prison.

They hadn't been in prison very long when they escaped by the way of the ventilation system and went on robbing banks. They came to be known as the Stopwatch Gang due to their precise planning and precision of being in and out in less than a minute. Their criminal activities went on until they were captured and returned to prison. This time, Patty devised a method of escape by saving cigarette butts and soaking them in water to get the nicotine juice from the tobacco and then swallowing a large quantity of it. This resulted in a very rapid heart rate. The guards were alarmed to the point that an ambulance was called. However, Paddy had arranged with help from the outside to have an ambulance waiting nearby so that when the real ambulance arrived to pick him up, he had already been picked up by his own pre-arranged ambulance.

He and I corresponded by letter three or four times yearly - mainly discussing horse racing news. I will leave this subject now as his history is already in book form. One thing I always admired about him was he never owned nor carried a gun.

• • •

When I first started my practice in Shawville and started receiving calls I was amazed at the vastness of the area I was to cover. For instance on my very first day I received a total of four calls. One was to Luskville which was 25 miles to the east, the next call was to the north to Alumette Island, more specifically Chapeau where Father D. J. Harrington, the parish priest, had a very large herd of beef cattle in close proximity to the Roman Catholic Church. This was 25 miles north from Shawville. What I am trying to say is that the two calls were 50 miles apart, and since I had to go up and back and down and back to do the two calls, I travelled 100 miles. It is obvious then that when I state that I drove an average of 50 to 60 thousand miles each year and wore out one, or sometimes two, cars a year that I am not exaggerating.

Another of those first calls was from a lady who said that she had received word from her husband in the barn that they had a cow having a cough. Since I did not think this was top priority I meant to leave it off for an hour or so as I proceeded on another call. However, a more urgent request came from the same lady to say that she hoped I could come as soon as possible as the cow was in distress.

There is an amusing side to this call because when I arrived it was obvious that we were dealing with a different story on the nature of the original call, because the cow was having difficulty delivering a calf. I apologized to the farmer that I had misinterpreted the nature of the call, because I thought she had said *cough* instead of calf. The farmer bent over backwards laughing and then said that his wife was a war bride and her British dialect sure sounded like *cough* instead of *calf*. I took the farmer's invitation to come with him to the house and meet his lady and we laughed about the situation while we had tea.

At the same time she said, "Oh doctor, would you look at my canary as she is having difficulty perching on her roost and is spending most of her time sitting on the floor of the cage." I told her that I did not have much training in avian medicine, however I would have a look. As I picked up the bird, the lady said to me, "Oh my dear doctor, with those big hands make sure you don't crush my bird." I told her I would be careful and it was very obvious the problem was that the bird's toenails were so long that they were curled and hence it could not sit on the roost. With a pair of scissors I gave the canary a pedicure and upon releasing it into the cage it immediately flew to its roosting bar. The lady declared me a hero and reimbursed me with a nice hug when I said there was no charge.

Incidentally this farmer had served with much distinction as a Royal Canadian Air Force fighter pilot in the Second World War. While in England he married his wife who had served in the British Royal Air Force as an airplane mechanic. He later became my pilot on the many trips into the bush camps to treat horses.

• • •

It seems that the winters when I first started practice were much more severe than they are at the present time. More particularly I remember one night very well.

I had just gone to bed at nine o'clock in the evening when the phone rang. It was a local farmer informing me that one of his cows had prolapsed her uterus following the birth of her calf. It was one of those evenings when the temperature was thirty degrees below zero and with a drifting wind seemed even colder. The roads in the area were not looked after as well as they were in later years and on this particular evening they were almost blocked with six-foot-high banks on either side.

When I got to the farmer's gateway it was obvious that his laneway was not snow plowed which meant that I had a long walk carrying all the equipment needed to complete the task that lay ahead of me. Since it was so cold I left my car running and hoofed it, first to the house. The house and barn had no electricity and, let me tell you, the conditions were very primitive and sanitation could have been improved.

The farmer and I proceeded to the barn with a lantern, a pail of cold water and a used hand towel. The conditions in the barn were atrocious to say the least as the ceiling was very low and there was very little distance between the back of the cow in distress and the wall. I stripped off my clothes to the waist, gave her a spinal anesthesia to stop her pressing while I was attempting to invert the uterus into position.

Without going into much detail, I completed the job and cleaned myself the best way I could. We returned to the house to warm up, however the house seemed to be colder than the barn. The rest of the family was huddled around the cookstove to keep warm. They had a pet duck in the house and he was standing on one leg at a time because obviously the floor was too cold.

I got paid for my services and booted back out to the car. Since I had left the car running it was as warm as toast and I soaked in the heat for a few minutes. When I put the car in gear and attempted to go home it would not go forward because the heat from the muffler had caused the brake drums to freeze in position. I had to use the tire wrench and bang on the drums to loosen them. Since, as I said previously, the road was semi-blocked it was too narrow to turn and I had to drive ahead some three or four miles to the next village in order to have enough clear space to turn.

I did eventually get home and had a blast of scotch and water before having a shower and returning to my bed.

The next morning when I awoke and tried to speak to my wife I discovered I had lost my voice to quinsy. It was six in the morning when another call came in and, as I was unable to talk, my wife had to answer the phone. It was another emergency which fortunately was only three miles out of the village, but the road was blocked solid. We were informed that the farmer was on the way with a horse and cutter to pick me up.

The cow had a condition called milk fever. This is a condition that occurs in high producing bovines when there is a tremendous flow of calcium from the bloodstream into the udder, and since calcium is needed for muscle metabolism, the cow goes into a state of paralysis that results in death in approximately 12 hours so there is little time to waste. The treatment consists of an intravenous injection of 16 ounces of calcium gluconate solution, and the cow invariably is up and on her feet in minutes.

The reason I mention this particular case is because after I had started the intravenous and it was running steadily I asked the farmer to hold up the bottle while I lay down in the manger as I was not feeling the best after the previous night's episode. Just about that time a couple of people came in to witness the event and somehow or other they began the rumour that I had a bit too much to drink and was lying down on the job. That rumour, however, was quelled in short order by my client who was a class individual. He reprimanded the individuals sincerely when he found out who started it.

There is an old saying, that sometimes life gets tasteless, don't it?

• • •

One of my first clients was a farmer who had emigrated from Germany as a very young man. For the following 15 to 20 years he worked with one or two farmers in the area until he had saved enough money to purchase a farm. After viewing a number of available properties he purchased a 100-acre farm with buildings that needed a lot of repair. He worked tirelessly to put the place in livable condition. I don't know much about his financial situation but he obviously must have taken a mortgage because at the same time as he purchased the property he also bought a few head of cattle and machinery to work the farm.

The cattle he had purchased were not of the highest quality and hence their milk production was below average. I suggested to him that he should purchase a high quality bull to enhance the value of future production. Just about that time the use of artificial insemination became available in the area and it was operated out of my practice with the help of technicians and myself actually doing the insemination. The semen from all available breeds was forwarded to us by bus from Kemptville, Ontario, where, of course the resident sires were all of the highest quality.

The gentleman agreed to advance in this direction and use the available sires from the unit. It is only natural that all of the farmers using the unit were hoping to obtain heifers rather than bull calves, because that was the only way they were going to increase production in their herds. It was with this concept in my mind that caused me to misinterpret the following requests.

Many times when I bred a cow for this gentleman he would say, "I want this to be a heifer," and, thinking he was making an effort to be humorous, I would jokingly reply, "Of course that is what you're going to get."

When the calves started to arrive they were approximately 50% female and 50% male. The farmer seemed upset and I thought it was about that, but then it did not take long for me to realize that what he had been doing was asking me to breed his poorer cows to the Hereford beef breed so that he could sell the calves for veal.

However when his better cows were bred to the superior Holstein bulls from the unit he got much better quality calves and consequently his herd improved. In the end it turned out to my advantage and to his, as some of the calves born off the cows which he determined to be inferior (and had asked me to breed them with Hereford semen) actually had Holstein heifer calves which turned out to be far superior to their mothers, so all was not lost.

What I learned from this was that one should be careful when listening to people with different dialects than your own. If there is any difficulty in understanding the pronunciation of the word then it should be clarified.

During the many dialogues I had with this gentleman he informed me that he was going to re-roof his barn and was having trouble obtaining the necessary metal sheets locally so he had gone to a large hardware store in Hull to obtain some after having read their advertisement in *The Citizen*.

When he arrived at the store's order desk he was informed that the person responsible was away for lunch but would be back in an hour. With that information he decided to have lunch himself and he went to the *Ottawa House* to eat. While he was there he met two gentlemen, and after 10 or 15 minutes' conversation he discovered that they were actually in the roofing business and it was rather coincidental that he was in town for the purpose of acquiring metal. The long and short of the situation was that he made a deal with them for delivery of the metal and paid for it in advance. Unfortunately my poor friend in his trusting manner had met the wrong people and it was an expensive experience as the metal for his barn never arrived.

He eventually did get his roofing material from a local supplier and the barn did get re-roofed with a lot of local help from neighbours who had heard of his experience and pitched in collectively to get the job done.

One day my client called to say that he had decided to return to Germany to make contact with his former girlfriend who had promised she would wait for him until he had established himself in Canada. He informed me also that he had made arrangements with another person to look after the farm while he was away for two to three weeks, and that he had told him that if there were any problems to call me.

Apparently after he arrived in Germany he found out that his girlfriend had got tired of waiting and was married. After a short search for a suitable lady to return to Canada with him, he was successful and was duly married. They arrived in Canada and eventually had two children, a boy and a girl. From my observation it was obvious that his new bride had adapted to the farming situation very well and was very proficient in both the kitchen and outside work.

I might add that my farmer client was very efficient with the production of a home brew, made from a potato or apple base, but only for his personal and limited use. However, after many a late night call I was the recipient of a few drams, effective, but not the best tasting.

• • •

During my time in Shawville my practice mainly involved the treatment of large animals. However, I did do a considerable amount of small animal work. Most of it in the surgical areas of castrations in males, and spaying female dogs and cats, which is the removal of the uterus and ovaries to prevent reproduction.

Further, all of the shots for disease prevention was carried out on specific evenings during the week when I was not tied up with the racing schedules. Needless to say, I was also available for injuries such as when dogs were hit by cars and farm vehicles, or got in front of mowers cutting hay and having a leg partly or totally severed. This meant having the leg attended to on the operating table, and on many occasions, ending with a three-legged dog carrying on with its life on the farm.

I was not, however, prepared for the run-of-the mill ailments in small animals, not having the necessary specialized equipment and further believing I needed more experience and training to make a proper professional diagnosis. Consequently, I invariably re-directed these cases to clinics in Ottawa.

In one case, however, I recall a woman phoning me about her middle-sized dog which was continually vomiting any food she had given it, but otherwise seemed happy. I asked her to bring it in and I would check it. After a normal examination I informed her I could not see any problem except for obvious dehydration. I could not rule out internal problems so I suggested that she take it to one of the clinics in Ottawa.

Three days later she called me to say she had taken the dog to an animal clinic in the city and it had been diagnosed as suffering from severe gastritis. However, the medicine that had been prescribed was now being vomited, too. As a last resort, I said that the only other thing I could do was to take a look inside by way of an incision. She agreed to this and immediately brought the dog back in.

This procedure was carried out and *lo and behold* there was an enlargement just two inches into the intestine from where it was attached to the stomach. It was obviously a foreign body.

Surgically, I removed some of the intestine along with the foreign object as there had been some necrosis. Incidentally, the object was a golf ball and it was surprising that the dog had been able to swallow such a large article. Of course, dogs have always had the ability to swallow large chunks of meat, so they obviously have a very accommodating oesophagus.

In joining the two ends of the intestine together I used a three-inch piece of dry cannelloni inserted into the lumens of the intestine to hold the two collapsible ends, spread out, while I pulled them together and sutured them. *The theory behind this was that as the sutured ends healed together the pasta would soften and make its way through the intestinal tract.* The abdominal incision was closed, and I was proud that I was able to help. On the two or three later occasions when I ran into the owner she reported that the dog had fully recovered and was happily running around attending to its dog business.

• • •

I would like to discuss the rather serious problem that exists regarding the indiscriminate use of antibiotics by people with little scientific knowledge, including the farmers. Within the last few years certain antibiotics have been available at lay sources such as feed mills. Certain farmers, in an attempt to avoid the cost of a veterinarian, will use the drugs on the wrong condition, actually where antibiotics are not warranted, hence adding insult to injury.

A case in point, a certain cow had a rather severe allergic reaction to something and had distressing signs of sneezing and coughing and nasal discharge. This is a case where antibiotics are not indicated but the farmer administered high dosages of penicillin and sulfa drugs over a three-day period. The cow eventually went off her feed, which means she stopped eating for a few days. The farmer called me as a last resort. After extensive examination I couldn't find one thing wrong with the animal except when using the stethoscope there were no intestinal sounds. She went a whole week without any interest in eating although she did drink water. After questioning the farmer extensively I found out about the antibiotic and sulfa treatments and determined that what he had done resulted in total destruction of all natural bacteria in the stomach.

The only treatment for this is the introduction of natural bacteria into the stomach and this is done by obtaining from a slaughterhouse the liquid contents of the rumen (one of three stomachs of a cow) which is loaded with natural and necessary bacteria to aid digestion. I made arrangements at Canada Packers to obtain the same and the farmer went to pick it up. The contents were administered by stomach tube and within 24 hours the cow was back on full feed.

The problem of indiscriminate use of drugs in veterinary practice still exists. Many veterinarians, including myself, have stayed away from the use of antibiotics in cases where they were actually indicated, believing that under certain conditions a case is better handled by letting the individual animal fight its problem with its own in body defense system (its immune system). We often feel that if we start with antibiotics too soon then the animal's system is going to, in effect say, "OK if you are going to fight my condition for me then I will leave it up to you and I won't bother." In cases such as this, however, we would support their problem with intravenous solutions of energizing supplements.

• • •

Another condition which occurs in cattle that may be of interest to readers not familiar with cattle problems is Hardware Disease. All bovines have a three-department stomach. The first is the rumen which is a large tank so to speak and cattle and another ruminants just figuratively *wolf* their roughage into them; this roughage goes into the said rumen without being chewed up and is there to soak and soften up. The animal then flips up a big wad and chews it thoroughly, which is called *chewing their cud.* Then it is swallowed and this goes into the second department where it is further roughed up before passing to the third stomach which is much like ours where acids are added to aid fermenting prior to going on into the intestines to be absorbed for energy and milk supply.

Problems may start if there are nails or any pieces of wire in the original roughage. This metal sinks to the bottom of the first stomach which anatomically is in close proximity to the heart on the other side of the diaphragm, which is the division between the food area and the lungs and heart.

Now and then a farmer may call and say, "My cow has a hump on her back and is off-feed and grunting, obviously in pain." This to a veterinarian is an indication that a piece of wire or nail may have pierced through the rumen wall and the diaphragm and is touching the pericardium *(outside cover)* of the heart. We can use a simple metal detector to confirm the presence of metal and that, along with a greatly accelerated heart rate, helps us make a diagnosis.

The treatment is a laparotomy of the flank, which involves making an incision and bringing the rumen to the open site and incising it large enough to have room to reach in at full arm's length to pull the hardware out and then sewing up the incision. Some antibiotics may be required to guard against infections. This operation is quite common in large animal practice where farmers inadvertently throw away nails and pieces of wire when fencing and the discarded metal ends up in the hay. Humourously, I once found a piece of metal that was lost from a milking machine which answered the question of how and where it got to.

• • •

Many so-called blessings come with a curse firmly attached. Pesticides can be classed in that category. From the earliest of times the common house or barn fly has been a perpetual annoyance in barns and country homes. In 1939 the use of DDT as an effective insecticide was discovered and it was used in the second half of World War II to control malaria and typhus among civilians and troops. After the war, DDT was made available for use as an agricultural insecticide and its production and use duly increased. Many farmers breathed a sigh of relief as now their homes and barns could be free of flies. What was not taken into consideration was the fact that something that was so efficient at killing flies could possibly be harmful to other forms of life.

One evening in September, 1960 I had a call from a farm woman who lived just south of the village telling me that their cows were just dropping dead in the field. I immediately went to the farm and, sure enough, there were dead cows lying in the field and others in extreme distress.

Upon questioning the farmer said that after milking he had sprayed around the stable and also had sprayed a bit on some of the cows so that they would be less annoyed by the heel flies. I asked to see the can and saw what I had suspected when he first mentioned the spray. It was spray intended for buildings only which was in a very high concentration and when it was absorbed through the cow's hide it attacked the nervous system causing paralysis and death. Six cows died and other cows which had only got a light dusting survived, but never returned to full health. A heartbreaking and expensive lesson.

I might add that I personally had experience with DDT during my active service with the army. Now and then, due to the fact that showers or baths were just a historical memory, we occasionally contracted body lice, and probably the so-called *BO*. Then someone from medical staff would come around and come up to us and say, "Loosen your belt." Then he would put the neck of a large puffer down the back of our collars and with one shot the DDT dust went down and out our trouser bottoms. Death to the bugs and an end to scratching!

• • •

Historically there has always been an awareness of the disease called rabies *(hydrophobia)*, even as far back as the early 1800s. For example, in the summer of 1819, the Duke of Richmond, the Governor General of British North America, was bitten on his hand by a fox. The injury apparently healed and he continued on with his duties. It was during a visit to the settlements on the Rideau that the first symptoms of rabies appeared and then the disease developed very rapidly. As he was in extreme agony his party had to stop at a barn close to the settlement that had already been named Richmond in his honour. It was there that he died on August 28th in that same year. The disease was not widespread at that time or for many years following so it was not something that was foremost in the minds of veterinarians when diagnosing illnesses.

In my college and budding-veterinarian days I listened to many lectures from professors over the four-year period. One thing that was drilled into us time and time again was to be good listeners. Also to not be afraid to ask lots of questions and above all to be very, very observant from the time you arrive until the time you leave on every call. I remember one professor saying, for instance, that when it came to nervous conditions in any animal, to be very aware of the possibility of rabies as nervous symptoms are an early sign of that disease. Although there were no cases in domestic animals at that time *(1950)*, it was known to exist in wildlife in the Arctic areas of Canada, and it was only a matter time before it would spread south as the disease was carried by these creatures which were always on the move.

With this warning always in the back of my mind I went to see a horse in one of the lumber camps in northern Quebec. Upon arrival I witnessed the animal, obviously in deep distress, staggering and walking in wide circles, and at one point walking up to a building used for storing hay, then pressing on the wall and pushing until he could walk right through it. This horse was obviously beyond veterinary care and it soon fell down in a comatose state. I realized that this was a possible rabies case.

Rabies is one of Canada's reportable diseases, which by law a veterinarian must report to the federal Department of Agriculture. As I suspected rabies in this case in northern Quebec, I reported it without delay so officials could come and take the animal's head for a brain pathologic study. This turned out to be the first diagnosed case of rabies in eastern Ontario or western Quebec. Consequently I was called on to speak at many local veterinary meetings to establish awareness of the existence of rabies and to outline safety procedures that should be taken.

Even with all the precautions that I preached about, I accidentally came in direct contact with the disease on three different occasions as the incidence of positive cases increased dramatically in my area. This was because my practice was in close proximity to the Quebec bush area, from whence the disease spread south.

Speaking of the three cases I came into contact with, let me describe them. The first was the case of a dog owner bringing me a sick dog in a small carrier kennel for examination. Without thinking, I started to remove the dog from its kennel when it immediately bit me on the hand. As mentioned above we had been told hundreds of times at university to ask lots of questions before acting, which obviously should have been done before I attempted to examine the dog. After further questioning, a case of rabies was suspected. The pathologic testing confirmed that it was positive and I was subjected to the 14 daily injections of anti-rabies serum into the abdominal muscle to offset the infection which if left unattended meant certain death.

The second case came after a long day's work when I was about to call it a day. The call came from a farm in Campbell's Bay about 20 miles west to attend to a cow which the farmer said had a can stuck in its mouth. I responded right away as I knew from past experience that there was no power in the barn where the cows were tied. As we ventured into the barn with him holding a coal oil lantern he pointed out the cow. I proceeded to her head and took a firm hold of her lower jaw with my right hand and proceeded to examine her mouth with my left. I found no can and, stupidly, one more time I was acting without asking questions. When it was later confirmed that the cow had rabies the *good doctor* was subjected to the 14-daily treatment series again.

The final and third time was when I was called to another farm to examine another cow. This time I had asked all the necessary questions and determined it almost certainly did have rabies. When I was informing the farmer that the cow would be examined by the federal inspectors, all of a sudden the cow bawled out loudly while flinging her head up in the air. Her saliva inadvertently landed partly on my outstretched hand which had a small scratch. Hence, once more I was subjected to the 14 once-a-day treatment.

Today veterinarians or anyone else at risk can receive preventive vaccination against rabies.

A good thing about rural communities at that time was that news travelled very quickly on the *gossip grapevine* which was efficiently facilitated by party telephone lines. And so it was with the information about the prevalence of rabies in the area. Almost everyone knew of the dangers of the disease and was on the look-out for any signs in their livestock or pets.

Early one Monday morning in 1967 I got a call from a very concerned woman asking my advice. Her husband had just come in from the barn and told her that one of the kittens in the barn had been acting very strangely, snarling and snapping at him so he had hit it on the head with a shovel to kill it, and then buried it. She was immediately on high alert as their two young grandchildren, aged four and six, had just been visiting from Nepean, Ontario and had been playing with that very kitten. I told her that she was right to be alarmed and that a federal veterinarian would be right down to the farm to pick up the kitten. This was done and a positive result for rabies was received within 24 hours.

The system quickly sprang into action. I was later told by the mother of the two boys that within minutes of hearing of the problem she had a call from the Medical Director of Health in Nepean asking her who her family doctor was, and informing her that appointments would be set up for the boys to go in for the anti-rabies vaccine shots starting that same day. Shortly after that she had a call from her family doctor to say that the boys were to go in at 5 p.m. each day for the 14 daily injections of anti-rabies serum. It is this type of coordination between provinces and medical jurisdictions that prevented many tragedies from occurring. I might add that the farmer and his wife also received the vaccine.

On Hallowe'en night in the fall of 1966, a small puppy died of rabies at my mother's farm residence. Shortly before the puppy died, three of my brothers and their young families had visited the farm and while there, had played with the puppy. As a result all the participants, including my pregnant sister-in-law, took the anti-rabies serum treatment over a two week period.

Unfortunately, not everyone receiving the 14-day anti-rabies serum was prevented from becoming infected. One young girl in the area had been infected by a rabid cat. She took the serum at about the same time as my brothers' families but died a few months later.

The disease was rampant for years and I and many veterinarians held wholesale vaccination clinics on specific advertised dates and times in community centres in towns and villages where people brought their animals to be immunized. Now, *in 2014,* the disease has been almost eradicated in Ontario and Quebec because of ingenious droppings of baited oral-devised vaccine by way of aircraft to the areas inhabited by wild animals.

An interesting fact about rabies is that until the virus reaches the brain there are no symptoms whatsoever. The virus travels to the brain by way of the nervous system so if the person or animal is bitten in the face the route to the brain is relatively short, possibly as little as a week. If the subject is bitten on the toe or foot then the time to reach the brain could be long. In some reported cases it has taken as long as a year to travel the distance to the brain. The virus is only transmitted by the saliva of a live animal but it will not survive outside of the body for any length of time. Therefore the reservoir of the disease is in a living animal.

• • •

In some cases regarding calls to the bush camps for the treatment of horses, access to the two closest camps where horses were working could be done by car. Mr. Ken Smith was the manager of most of the lumber companies in the area and as he also lived in Shawville, he accompanied me on one particular call to treat a horse that had been severely injured by way of puncturing its abdomen in a rather peculiar manner.

As it was walking down the trail where sleighs are extensively used, one of the sleigh stakes, which are used as uprights to hold logs in place on the load, had fallen off a previous sleigh and was lying on the ground. The horse stepped on one end of the stick with his right foot, causing the stick to flip up and hit him on the belly, at which point he immediately jumped forward and the stake was then forced into a perpendicular position. When the horse came down the stake penetrated the animal to the point where it came out about a foot above its back.

When I got there the animal was in a distressed situation and sweating. I immediately did a rectal examination and to my surprise the stick had entered the bottom part of the animal's belly but was lateral to the actual stomach wall. It had stayed mostly intramuscular on the inside of the leg and had missed the main femoral artery and extended up and, as I have already stated, it came out its back.

I said to Mr. Smith in a rather humorous manner, "They never told me at veterinary college how to handle cases like this."

With a man standing at the horse's head I tied a rope to the piece protruding out its back and tied it to a branch overhead. With one of the men's chainsaws we cut off the bottom part which was sticking out of the bottom of the animal, leaving only enough length to tie a bed sheet to it. We soaked the sheet with healing oil and slapped the horse on the back side. As as he jumped forward the stick came flying out and then we used the sheet which was attached to the end of it and was still inside the horse to see-saw back and forth to clean the wound before pulling it out. In this case antibiotics were administered and the horse made an uneventful recovery.

It seems that there is always something amusing attached to all serious problems. On this call we spoke with the clerk and bookkeeper at the lumber camp who was a man in his 30s and spoke English with a thick French accent.

Mr. Smith asked this gentleman how things were going and he said, "Oh Mr. Smit, for me dare it is lonesome up here and wish you find for me a nice lady come here wit me." Mr. Smith replied, "You know what, Joe there's a young lady I know and she would be excellent for you - also she has a child so you wouldn't have to bother trying get babies." The immediate response was, "Oh Mr Smit for me dare I like dat bodder, me."

• • •

I recall a request by telephone from Mr. Hobbs informing me that he had a cow having difficulty delivering her calf. I responded immediately and asked my son Mickey if he wished to accompany me, and he jumped into the car.

When I examined the animal it was obvious that the calf was too big for natural delivery and that a cesarean section was in order. After we had anesthetized the cow and proceeded with the operation it was obvious that the farmer was going to be of no help because on the sight of the first blood his natural complexion had changed to a rather green shade and he backed away from being the assistant I needed to hold the intestines in place while I pulled the uterus to the incision site. Since things were at a critical stage I said to my 14-year-old son, "Come here boy, wash your arms and get here fast." I must praise him because he stepped right up and got his arms right into the incision and followed my instructions to hold back the intestines. Although I must say it was amusing to see his eyes shut so tight and his face in a distorted grimace, but he stayed on the job until the calf was delivered alive and healthy.

The reason I bring this story to light, even though this type of delivery happened many times, is that I think he reminds me yearly if not more often, saying, "Dad, do you remember the time when I helped you....? "

• • •

One afternoon I received a call from the parish priest in Kazabazua which was approximately 50 miles from my office. To get there you go down highway 148 to Beechgrove, turn left and go right over the Laurentian Hills. He told me that a parishioner of his had a Jersey cow which just had a calf and was now paralyzed and nearly dead.

Immediately I diagnosed it as having milk fever, and as I mentioned once before in describing a case, there is a tremendous flow of calcium from the bloodstream to the udder, and since calcium is essential for muscle metabolism, including the heart, it has to be treated within 12 hours or there is death. He told me that someone would be waiting at the hotel in the village who would go with me to the farm.

After arriving at my rendez-vous we proceeded down a long lane which I must say was unfit for a low-level car. Since I knew what was going to be required for treatment I had a 16-ounce bottle of calcium gluconate which had to be warmed to body temperature. As I waited for it to warm I recall there were several children in the house with their mother. She informed me that her husband was away in the lumber camp for the winter and would be home sometime in April. This was November so I realized that the total responsibility for the family and the farm was lying heavily on her shoulders.

We proceeded to the barn with one or two children in tow and when I arrived the cow was in a recumbent position with the family bible opened over its back and a rosary around its neck with two reeds in the form of a cross.

The lady jumped to remove the material and I said to her, "No, don't do that. We are going to need whatever help we can get and a little prayer won't hurt." Immediately she instructed her children and she, herself, knelt down to pray as I proceeded with the intravenous introduction of the calcium solution.

I might add that the results of treatment are very dramatic, and as in ninety-nine per cent of cases the cow was on her feet within ten minutes and ready to eat hay.

At this point the lady said, "Oh thank you God and, of course, you too, Sir, this is almost a miracle." We returned to the house at which point she informed me that she had no money but promised that in the spring when her husband came home she would come to my office and pay the bill. With that I headed for home with the feeling that this was one case that I could mark down to charity. I must say that we have to do this once in a while because not everyone is as fortunate as many of us.

Some five months later a car arrived at the front of my office and in a few moments a lady came to the door. I remember she had a long purse hanging from her hand and was dressed entirely in black. She said, "Hello Doctor, I've come to pay my bill." I did not have the slightest idea as to who she was so I excused myself for a moment and went into the house proper and said to my wife, "There's a lady out here to pay a bill and I wonder if you might know who she is." Mary took a casual look in and signalled that she didn't know her. Then I had to ask her name, and she immediately informed me that she was the person with the very sick cow at Kazabazua last fall.

My immediate feeling was that wonders never cease, and without showing my surprise I changed her bill to a nominal amount and thanked her sincerely. She went on to thank me very much and informed me that the cow supplied milk for the whole family over the winter. I had never expected to see this woman again.

I must say that I felt good inside and that the whole experience had renewed my faith in humanity.

• • •

Up to this point we've spoken of individual cases, most of which we would consider from a veterinary standpoint to be 'fire engine calls' where there is a problem and they want service as soon as possible. What I want to discuss now is about a veterinary service termed herd health.

This is a contract between the veterinarian and the owner of a dairy-producing herd. Since all milk producing herds operate in Canada under a quota system whereby the farm produces a specific amount of milk daily and the money they receive for this quota brings top price.

It is important for the farmers to maintain this production at a constant level, neither too much nor too little. If they produce too much then the milk is paid for at a commercial price level, which is far lower than the normal. Of course if they don't produce enough milk to fulfill their quota then obviously they are losing money.

The contract they have with the veterinarian is to maintain this level of production and to have cattle that are healthy with no so-called empty stalls. In this case the veterinarian and the farmer maintain a rigid bookkeeping system and regular visits at the veterinarian's own time are made to determine the status of each and every cow. There is no longer the case of having a favoured cow Bessie who is kept as a pet. Every cow in the herd has to produce at her maximum at all times and, if for any reason whatsoever, she is unable to do that then they are culled and replaced immediately. All farmers in the dairy business have a backup supply of cattle derived from raising the heifer calves from birth.

Within two months of a cow having a calf she is re-bred usually by artificial insemination. It is the duty of the veterinarian during his regular visits to determine that the cow is pregnant. If she is determined negative in that respect she's bred again. If for some pathological reason the cow is unable to conceive then she is culled at the end of her normal lactation of nine months and replaced with one of the new heifers that is just beginning a lactation period.

Normal vaccinations and inspections are made to prevent normal diseases common to cattle, so that a healthy herd is always in place.

• • •

Regarding my contracts with the various lumber companies for treatment of horses, the only access was by float plane to many of the camps. Many of my visits to the camps, for whatever reason, were made in a Cessna 185 piloted by Iverson Harris who during the World War II was a fighter pilot who, as I mentioned earlier, served with noted distinction. Most of the trips were without any undue experiences and were considered routine. However, on some occasions we had to deal with rather tricky weather but we worked around those problems.

One time I said to Iverson that everybody is vulnerable and I would hope that if anything happened to him that I would be able to land the airplane in one of the many lakes that always seemed to be in view. Consequently, he showed me how to fly the plane level and flat by using the throttle and the steering wheel that controlled the flaps. Of course, I casually observed him as much as possible, particularly when it came time to land on the lake.

One day he said to me, "The weather is perfect and the conditions are right and I want to teach you how to land this aircraft on the lake." And as we approached the lake he said to me, "Okay, take over." I took the controls and took the plane down to make a landing, but I couldn't determine how far I was above the water. All of a sudden I was running out of distance on the lake and was coming to the end and was still not on the water so he immediately took over taking the plane up again to make a circuit.

Iverson said, "I just want to tell you not to feel too bad because no one could land the plane without using some type of guide, and I let you do it, intentionally without instruction." When we made the circuit and were ready to land again he said, "I want you to view the side of the lake with your right eye and use the trees as a guide to indicate how far above the water you are, and as you approach the lake just lower the plane until you run out at the bottom of the tree line and you'll be on the water within a few feet." I tried this twice and eventually made landing, a little skimpy, but otherwise okay, and I felt that if there was ever an emergency at least I would be able to get the plane down.

Every year I always had a senior student from the university come and spend the summer with me for experience. They lived with us in the house as one of the family. One student was only with us for a few days when we had a call to one of the lumber camps and he came along in the backseat in the airplane. We had to do work at two different camps and after finishing the first one, both the weather and time got a little *iffy* but Iverson felt we could make the second leg in time, while we still had light.

We flew north along the Coulonge River at a relatively low level as a guide from one lake to the other. As we came in close proximity to the lake we wanted to land on we experienced some fog, and since we were at the point of no return, we continued on and into a very complete whiteout of dense fog. At that point my stomach was in a *wee* bit of a knot and I felt we were in trouble. Here is where experience on the part of the pilot takes over. Having been up and down this little river hundreds of times he knew exactly where we were. I saw him look at his watch and he mumbled, maybe to give us some comfort, that we were about 30 seconds from the lake. At that point I glanced in the backseat and my student friend was exhibiting some apprehension also.

We felt the plane going down, down, down, and finally the sound of touching water was the best feeling I have had for a long time. Even Iverson let out a deep blast of air showing his relief. At this point normally the pilot increases the throttle to stay on the step, so to speak, which means you don't let the airplane pontoons sink deep into the water and you can continue faster until you get to the docking point on the lake. This time, however, because of the deep fog he let plane pontoons sink into the water and we came to rest. We fiddled around for some 30 minutes before we could find the dock visually and the rest of the trip was uneventful.

Another time Iverson called me and said that he was flying two Americans into a fish camp and he asked if I would like to come along if I was not busy. I said I would meet him at the river at the pickup point. After all passengers were onboard we took off, later landing on Bell Lake and tying up at the dock. The two Americans disembarked first and I handed their gear and luggage out to them. There was one kit bag that had the name I. A. Harris # W23742 RCAF on it. I turned to Iverson who was still in the pilot's seat adjusting the airplane for permanent shutdown and asked, "Where do you want me to put your kit?" He said, "What kit, I have nothing here." At this point I said, "Well your name is on it."

Iverson turned around and looked at the bag and was aghast. He asked one of the Americans where he got that bag and he answered that he had purchased it in a war surplus store in Boston. Iverson said, "The last time I saw that bag was on the Queen Elizabeth when we were returning home after the war. We had to turn our flying suits back to authorities as we were not allowed to take them home. Since I had sold my suit beforehand in England, I stuffed a blanket into the bag and turned it in to the quartermaster on deck."

The American gave the bag back to Iverson and I sent the story to *Believe it or Not* in the Readers Digest for publication.

• • •

Shawville, Quebec is situated in the centre of Pontiac County and was previously known as Clarendon Center with a population of between 1500 and 2000 people. This village and the surrounding area, known as Clarendon Township, was settled by a Colonel Clarendon, a British army officer in the early 1800s. The area was surveyed and divided into 100-acre lots with built-in road allowances. The Colonel was a staunch Protestant and he saw to it that these lands were settled only by Protestants and after a 100 acre plot of land was allocated to a specific person, it was written into the deed that if by devious or other means this land should fall into the hands of a Roman Catholic then the land would be sold and the price would be set by the two closest neighbours. This type of restriction, of course, would not be effective today, but that was the case then.

When I went to Shawville in 1951 there was only one Roman Catholic family in the village, Mel Kehoe, his wife and family, but they were followed by Benedict Allen and his family. Benedict worked as a salesman in the car business at Hodgins Chevrolet. When I left Shawville in 1970 that was still the status that existed among the population of 2000. There were five Protestant churches in town but the closest Catholic Church was some ten miles away in Bristol.

This ratio of Catholic to Protestant changed dramatically after the opening of the Bristol Iron Mines and The Pulp and Paper Mill at Portage du Fort when a large influx of workers and administrative families moved into the general area. Many farmers reduced the size of their operation and took jobs in either of the two companies.

• • •

I recall one incident when early in the morning a farmer called me and told me that he had a cow with milk fever and which was totally comatose in her stall. He said, however, that he was unable to stay around as he was working at the Bristol Iron Mine and had to go to work.

I realized the call was urgent and I told him I would be there as soon as possible and he need not stay as I could handle the case myself. This was the condition where if 16 ounces of calcium gluconate could be administered intravenously then there would be an immediate response and the cow invariably was on her feet in less than 15 minutes.

When I arrived at the farm the farmer had already left and I immediately began treatment of the animal. She responded very well but was still in a recumbent position. I attempted to get her up by standing in the gutter and lifting on her tail. As she started to rise she came backwards toward me. Since I was standing in the gutter I could not step backward fast enough and she came on top of me. I lay full length in the gutter with my face upward and directly behind the next standing cow.

There was absolutely no way I could move as the hindquarters of the cow were directly on top of me and, to make matters worse, the cow directly to the right of the affected cow and in front of my face decided it was time to defecate and I got the full treatment.

I might add there were no cell phones at that time and there was no way I could get help from anyone. I was very cognizant of the fact that not only was I in a bad situation but at any moment it could get much, much worse as the cow who had just given me my fecal facial could step back onto my head. I tried to encourage her to stay where she was by reaching over and tickling her heels. She would then immediately kick but her kicks went above me. Obviously she did not decide to step backward as I survived to relate this tale.

My dilemma was corrected only by a very observant farmer nearby who had driven by two hours earlier and noticed my car at this particular farm. I might add that every farmer in the area knew what type of vehicle I drove. Upon his return he saw my car was still there so he came in wondering if any help was needed.

Of course he found me in my precarious position. He was my saviour and I might add that I had to wear a body brace for some months after, due to a low back problem, the result of my time spent in the gutter with my cow-companion. Humorously, my problem was later noted by me as being one of many occupational hazards.

• • •

One could fill four books about all the different calls a veterinarian receives for advice and treatment during his life in practice, but a lot of them would be repetitious. However, cases such as the one reported by a feed-lot dealer who had lost two steers from a 30-head herd of cattle, is interesting. He asked me for immediate help if possible.

I went to the site and felt that from all the symptoms and answers to my questions it appeared that poisoning was involved. First things first: the feeding practice had to be checked right away. Realistically it meant removal of the cattle from the site until we we could discover the cause of the deaths. The feed appeared normal, but where was the source of the water? It was from a never-ending spring flowing from a ruptured overflowing drainage system that covered many farms. After much questioning and scouting around it was discovered that one mile away was a large potato-growing operation that used a bug control product called *Paris Green,* with the active ingredient being arsenic. It was discovered that several bags of it had been left over in the field after the harvest, and with the fall rains the product had become fluid and seeped down into the underground drainage system. This inadvertently, of course, ended up in the water coming to the surface in the feed lot.

The case was solved and corrections made all around - and here ends the outcome of just another of the many calls a veterinarian receives throughout his career.

• • •

While residing in Shawville I was acquainted with a very fine gentlemen who was held in very high esteem by everyone. He was generally known and recognized as living the almost perfect life. He neither drank nor smoked and attended church regularly, he set a very fine example for people to follow. His wife had died some years previous to my knowing him and he had a family all married and living elsewhere. He did have a housekeeper who stayed with him all week but went to her own home on the weekends.

One day I had a call from him asking me at my convenience to drop into his house as he had a matter he wished to discuss. I agreed, although I wondered what the subject might be. When I arrived we discussed the weather and other small talk until he finally asked me if he could take me into his confidence. Of course I readily agreed that he could. "I don't know how to start this, Roly, but I do once in a while take a small drink," he said, "you know my friend Joel who died recently always helped me in this regard, so that when I wanted a bottle of rye he would pick it up and deliver it to me. Since my housekeeper is away tomorrow I would appreciate it if you would pick up two large bottles of Seagrams Royal Deluxe and deliver them to me in a plain box. I will give you the money now." I again assured him of my confidence and went on my way.

Since it was two weeks before Christmas then, I also picked up a couple bottles for myself and delivered the same to him.

Every Sunday when I took my children to Sunday school I noticed his car was always missing because, of course, he was attending church. One Sunday as I was going by with the children I noticed his car was still in the yard. I paid little attention to that until on my return I noticed the car still there. This was Sunday and I knew that his housekeeper would be at her home, so after checking one more time and seeing that his car was still in the yard, I called his housekeeper and asked her if the gentleman was well and she assured me that he was. I explained to her that the car was still in the yard and he had not gone to church. She said she would check immediately and report to me.

Alas, when she arrived she found him dead in bed and she called me immediately. Although I thought of many things, I did think about the Rye that would be in his house and knew with respect for his wishes I'd better it get out of there before the public or the family would see it.

That evening, using a flashlight so as not to alert the neighbours I went to his home and checked everywhere the booze might be stashed. It must be in the basement I reasoned - I must say I looked for an hour and found nothing and wondered where the whiskey could be. Then I thought about the fact that that he burned coal in the furnace so I got a shovel and dug around in the coal bin until I came upon a box. On opening it, *lo and behold* there were the two bottles, one slightly used along with two bottles of ginger ale. I left the ginger ale but tucked the two bottles of Seagrams under my jacket and took them home with me, adding them to my own larder.

After the funeral, his family had gathered at their father's house and since they knew that I was involved, along with his housekeeper, in finding him deceased they invited me over. After I was introduced to them all, we sat down and the first thing one of his sons said very politely, "Dr. Armitage would you care to have a drink with us?" And, after my agreeing to partake, he pulled out a bottle of Crown Royal, poured everyone a drink. As we raised our glasses to the gentleman who had departed to be in the hands of the great architect of the universe, the son said to me, "Dr. Armitage we want to thank you very much for your support and the concern you showed regarding our dad and his passing, but I just want also to note one thing, this is the first bottle of whiskey that has ever been in this house." I like to tell this story because I am sure there are many many cases like this that have occurred.

• • •

When I first went to Shawville, the first house we rented was on the main street and it had running water but no inside toilet. We put up with this for the first year until we found the first available place with both indoor plumbing and a drilled well. Actually there were several residents still on the outdoor toilet system at the time.

Two years later we built our own bungalow on the east side of town and of course with a drilled well and indoor plumbing. I, however, remember on several occasions on breezy and misty mornings there was a rather unpleasant and odoriferous smell permeating our environment because of the numerous outdoor facilities that then existed in the village.

Shortly thereafter I was appointed to the position of sanitary inspector for the Pontiac County Health Unit and it became very obvious to me that something had to be done about establishing a sewer and water system for the village. I spoke to many people about the condition and that it was my intent to run for village council, for the sole purpose of bringing about the establishment of this project. I submitted my name for council, and at the next election I headed the polls which indicated to me that there was a distinct interest in doing something about this.

After a few council meetings we agreed to contact J. L. Richards and Associates to do a feasibility study on costs for the project. We were fortunate in having a bacteria free and constantly overflowing spring of tremendous volume at the east end of the village where many villagers gathered daily to collect clean water. Some months later Richards came forward with a tentative cost per square foot frontage of each lot and a determination of this assessment and how many years it would take to have the system paid for. In establishing this cost many more meetings were held with Richards, the townspeople, and with the local provincial government representative. It was established that generous grants were available from Quebec for this purpose, and finally a decision was made to proceed with the project. We put the project out for tender and a company was chosen to do the work. For a whole year there was much inconvenience and closed streets but everyone was very considerate and patient.

The water supply system consisted of pumps, water mains, hydrants and an overhead storage tank to develop pressure, while the sewage system also consisted of pumping stations, drainage lines, and two large holding tanks to purify the system. This involved the pumping of oxygenated air into the sewage which eventually brought about the destruction of bacteria so that the overflow into the existing creek was sterile and ended up in the Ottawa River. Shawville was the first community of that size, not only in the County of Pontiac but also in all of Western Quebec to have such an efficient and enviable system in existence.

• • •

Not everything from my time in Shawville was of a veterinary or municipal nature. One thing that happened every year was the Shawville Fair and without a doubt it was not only the largest fair in Pontiac County or Western Quebec, but in the whole Ottawa area it was considered first or second, competing only with the Carp Fair for recognition and attendance.

One outstanding performance was the so-called 'Road Class' entry in the horse show. This is a class within the horse entries that is usually held indoors and is comprised of trotters only. They are attached to a suitable and distinctive buggy and the speed and endurance of the horse and horsemanship on the part of the driver is exhibited. The horse must be kept on stride, which means staying *on gait* called trotting and not *breaking* which is when the horse goes off stride and gallops and is then disqualified.

The speed is electrifying actually when held in such close quarters with dirt flying off the wheels and the horses' hooves in close competition. One evening after one of those events in Shawville there was a gathering in one of the local hotels when the subject came up, of course after a few beers, as to the best horse and buggy in the road class. One very noted racing enthusiast put up a purse for the winner if the participants would partake in a midnight race from one end of town to the other and the winner would take all. It sounded good and everyone in attendance who had a horse suitable for the event agreed to have a GO at it.

We went to our respective stables and hitched up and reported to the west end of town at 3:00 a.m. It was agreed to have someone in attendance at each crossroads to avoid any collision with cars and that was organized. The finish line was at a specific spot at the east end of town where a designated judge would decide the winner.

A few minutes later the word GO was given and six horses and buggies raced all out with sparks flying off their steel on the pavement as an added attraction. Ultimately I was declared the winner and after my horse was put away I returned back to the hotel and received my winnings, and of course another beer and all the accolades from my friends.

I returned home where the reception was quite different.

My wife had witnessed the end of the event as the finish line was close to my house. The noise of the horses hooves on the concrete had not only awakened other people, she too was awakened and recognized my horse as I tore into the finish line. She realized that the race was not only the reason for my being late getting home, but that I was part of it all.

I had to tap on the door which was locked and I clearly recall Mary's remarks, "Roly, when are you going to grow up?" I didn't even know myself at that point, but the rest is history. The small number of people declaring annoyance about the race were outnumbered by the many people who said they were sorry not to have witnessed the event and, to this day, the race is still talked about in town.

• • •

I would like to discuss my association with the Shawville Fair. As I alluded to previously, the fair had always been recognized as not only the best fair in Pontiac

County but also in the whole Ottawa area. It was always a question about who had the best fair, Carp, Ontario or Shawville, Quebec. It became obvious that Shawville was greatly in need of an indoor show building that could also possibly be used as a hockey rink which was badly needed as the original rink, known as the *Richardson Arena*, had served a useful purpose but was totally in disrepair.

I was on the exhibition board in the early 1960s and eventually became the president. At the time horse racing was held at the track on the fairgrounds, as an attraction during the fair dates, but the time came when this had to move because of overcrowding and interference. *I will mention later about how a group got together and acquired new land near Yarm, just east of the village of Shawville for that purpose.* After much discussion at the board level we agreed to proceed with construction of a new arena to be brought about by selling debentures and a grant from the province. Also as a source of income to defray the cost, I personally arranged with every farmer I met to donate a calf and grow it up to be sold at an auction which was to be held in the fall. The response was fantastic and eventually the sale was held and a considerable amount of money was realized to be used for the new arena.

I also remember one major problem that arose. The Provincial Government had agreed to give us $25,000 towards the project and just before the fair was to open it was discovered that the province's offer was not $25,000 cash but $5,000 each year for five years which meant we were immediately short $20,000 to pay the fair opening bills. The problem was solved when Dr. S. E. McDowell put forward the $20,000 to pay the bill and took a mortgage on the property at a certain percent, which was duly honoured over the next few years. The money that we got by selling debentures was collected by offering 6% on $1000 loans and 5% on $500 loans.

I recall visiting one man, a bachelor living alone, and we discussed the possibility of a loan. He listened to the details and agreed to lend $2000 and immediately peeled back the oil cloth on his table where we were sitting and there was two vintage $1000 bills pressed neatly under it. When I took the money into the bank, the manager said he had not seen one of those ancient *items* for some time, but said they were still honoured by the government of Canada.

Without going into any more details, the building was not only built for $160,000 but it also had an artificial ice plant. Many the horse show has since been held in that arena and many hockey games have been won and lost. I might add that someone at the Chamber of Commerce must have thought that I had done a fairly good job as I was made *Citizen of the Year.* I remember telling them at the time that there was a hell of a lot more people involved than Roly Armitage in getting that job done.

• • •

Regarding the new 30 acres of lands acquired for the building of the so-called Shawville Driving Club in the early 1960s: we put the group together and agreed to build a new half-mile track with associated hub rail and stabling for 20 horses at an estimated cost of approximately $3000 per member. If my memory is half correct I remember some of the original people were Brent Horner, Barry Murray, Sterling Hobbs, *Bake Shop* Bill Horner, Red Young, Ebert Richardson, myself and others that this 90-year-old head won't come up with and I apologize for that because there were others who promoted the whole project which was an absolute success. We enjoyed many pleasant times training horses and partying along with the social aspects of many memorable race meets with large crowds. The Club is still in progress with many new members there now. Just last year I sold my share to a new member for the amount of my original investment.

• • •

After having been in General Veterinary practice in Shawville, Quebec from 1951 there came a time in 1969 when I felt a change had to be made for two reasons. First I had a growing desire to become more involved in the treatment of horses only and secondly the government of Quebec had become more involved in the methods by which farmers would have to pay for veterinary services.

One day a government representative came to my office and informed me during an hour-long dialogue that after January 1st, 1970 the most a veterinarian could charge the farmer was five dollars for a call and the remainder of the cost would be paid by the government. This meant making triplicate copies of each and every call. I remember my immediate response was that I was not in favour of this procedure, but the person who was laying out the details of the procedure informed me that I had no choice.

I informed the representative that I had always been an individual who made my own decisions and that there was no one in the world who knew better than myself how much my services were worth and that I intended to practise my profession in that manner henceforth. If that meant leaving the province to practise my profession, then I would do so. He told me that their direction was final and there was no elasticity.

The very next day my brother, who was a representative of a veterinary drug sales company, was in my office and I told him of the meeting I had with the Quebec government representative and informed him that my decision was to make a move and sell my practice. The word got around very quickly that my practice was for sale and within a week I had a call from a doctor in Ontario who had been an assistant in a large practice in Kingston. Without going into any detail my practice was sold; the doctor came to Shawville and as agreed I worked with him for three weeks prior to my departure.

Shortly thereafter I recall a very touching experience when a farewell party was held in my honour. I think everyone who l had ever been associated with during my time in Shawville was present to thank me and wish me well in my future.

With my dog, Smoky

CHAPTER 9 - RACING

That winter of 1970 my family and I rented a house in Dunrobin, Ontario while my new house and veterinary clinic were being built on our home farm which had been willed to me by my late uncle. All the things I dreamed about happening were coming to fruition as I built a 20-stall barn and a half mile training track and became deeply involved in treating, training, and breeding of standardbred horses.

Also, I was a local representative of the Canadian Trotting Association, one of some twenty representatives from different areas across Canada. Eventually I became the president of the 20,000-member Association as well as president of the Canadian Standardbred Horse Society. At the same time I established a rather large equine practice in the general Ottawa area with a senior student from the veterinary graduating classes coming to work with me mostly for experience each and every year. I also established an on-site clinic at the farm where many horses were brought to my place for treatment. This saved a lot of driving on calls but at the same time I did go to Rideau Carleton Raceway where I provided veterinary services.

• • •

The racetrack itself was established in 1963 and in the 1970s the track itself ran into rather difficult financial situations and went into receivership. While the track was in early receivership it was being managed by an appointed individual with no knowledge whatsoever of horsemanship or racetrack management. It was finally purchased by two entrepreneurs from Toronto, one a very knowledgeable and respected horseman and the other a very capable businessman.

On one occasion, since there was absolute disunity between the horseman on the track and the appointed track director, I felt that possibly I could be of some help in trying to coordinate some unity between the two groups, so I asked for an interview with the manager. This request was granted and we weren't long into the meeting when, after I had suggested some immediate solutions to the impasse, I was informed by the manager that if that was the purpose of the meeting then the meeting was terminated, and I left the room.

The following Sunday I was having breakfast in the cafeteria when I met one of the owners and explained to him how I'd been treated by the manager when my only purpose was to try to bring about better relations between the horsemen on the racetrack and management hoping that eventually this would establish a better horse racing atmosphere for the Ottawa area. He listened to what I had to say and, lo and behold, a couple of days later I got a call from him asking me if I would meet him at the Château Laurier Hotel, to which I agreed.

I had no idea what the meeting was to be about until shortly into our meeting he said let's get to the point right away and asked me if I was interested in managing the racetrack. This was the last thing I had expected to be offered. Right off the bat I said that I didn't think financially I could afford to put away my veterinary practice *black bag* to take on that duty. His immediate response was to try me with a very attractive remuneration figure. I had to give that opportunity some thought, and told him that I would consider his offer of employment but first of all I'd have to speak with my wife and family who would eventually be affected by my absence almost every evening. I said I would get back to him within 48 hours.

After discussing the situation with my family, I decided to give it a try, and went back to the principal owner and between the two of us we came up with an agreement.

We discussed at length what needed to be done immediately regarding staff and physical changes to the plant particularly in the backstretch or barn area where the buildings were in bad repair, and that a new horse racing paddock had to be built. Once we agreed on the type of structure for ten races to be housed at one time, we put the building description up for tender, and to our total amazement the lowest cost for construction was $600,000.

Of course this quote was far beyond our budget. Eventually with the help of several horsemen and one in particular who was a building contractor, we set about constructing the building ourselves. I knew lumber producers in the Shawville area and called upon them to supply the lumber necessary to get the job done.

I recall that shortly after the construction was halfway along a building inspector showed up from the Gloucester Council and asked for a building permit, which we did not have. He put in a stop order until a proper blueprint was in place. As my brother-in-law was an architect we soon, at no cost, came up with the necessary documents and proceeded with building the best ten-race paddock in Canada, bar none at that point. I might add that the final cost was less than $200,000, well within our budget.

The next thing we did was establish a working group between the horsemen and the track management. The group consisted of a driver, trainer, and a horse owner from the horsemen's side, and the race secretary, chief financial officer, paramutual officer and myself from the management side. This system worked harmoniously for several years as we mutually agreed on where money should be spent to enhance the image of the sport and attendance at the gate. I might add that the racetrack immediately went into a profitable position.

Digressing a bit, during my time as president of the Canadian Trotting Association I was approached by the insurance company involved in our policy regarding welfare of drivers during the races and was informed that we were going to have to increase our premium payments because of the large number of accidents occurring - in some cases a minimum of one to two deaths a year in North America. This increase in payment, of course, did not go down well with horsemen who eventually would have to pay the cost of the increased premium.

It was further established that the majority of the accidents were *hub rail* oriented, meaning that the accidents were being caused by the hub rail which was a small barrier designating the inside of the race track at the height of the hub of the wheel of the *sulky,* the vehicle on which the driver sat behind the horse. At times horses would be forced into this fence by another horse on the outside resulting in an accident where the horse and the driver went over the rail, and as mentioned previously, sometimes resulting in death or serious injury. Since the track hub rail was in very bad condition and needed to be replaced at a cost of $60,000, I questioned why we had a hub rail in the first place and thought about removing it and replacing it with upright white and easy-to-see rubber pylons at intervals in its stead. The thinking was that if a horse was forced into the infield that there would be no obstacle to cause an accident and if during a race a driver tried to shortcut by going inside these pylons they would be disqualified. To bring this all about I went to the racing commission in Toronto and put forward my suggestion. Immediately the response was that you simply can't run a race without a hub rail which was of course like everything in life - it is difficult to accept change. Eventually after repeated requests on my part the commission allowed me to remove the hub rail as I had suggested, but that I would be responsible for its consequences. Without further discussion about this issue I might add that there is not a racetrack in the world with a hub rail today and each and every one has rubber pylons instead. To my knowledge there have been no deaths in the past ten years.

May I humbly state that as a result of this very important change I was nominated and accepted into the Canadian Horse Racing Hall of Fame. I will conclude this portion on my attachment to the Rideau Carleton Raceway by stating that I remained the president for 10 years until my retirement and entry into the political field.

• • •

As mentioned earlier, from 1976 to 1980, during my term of office as president of the Canadian Trotting Association with its head office in Toronto, more particularly Mississauga, I visited every one of the 46 racetracks in

Canada, as well as the majority of standardbred race tracks in the world.

It is customary for every country to host an international meeting for presidents to discuss mutual problems. One problem that existed was that every country had their own way of identifying a specific horse. We in Canada had a tattoo number issued upon registration of the foal's birth, and this tattoo was placed on the upper lip by a registered technician. Freeze brands on the neck and under the mane was the method of identification in Australia and New Zealand, while France, Holland, and Italy had variants of pictures and tattoos on the horse, and in some places no identification at all except the word of the breeder that the horse was the offspring of a certain mare and that a certain stallion was its father. In any case, it was proven many many times that falsehoods existed in the breeding industry.

At one of those international meetings in France we were to agree on a universal method of identification and we selected the freeze brand method. A few years later at another conference the method of ensuring the authenticity of the true breeding of a foal was established by making DNA data mandatory for all mares and stallions in the breeding industry. This was to be put on record internationally. Now when the foal is born, the owner notifies the existing record keepers in each country declaring who the father and mother of the foal is, which is followed up by a technician coming to the farm and taking a blood test of the foal to authenticate the breeding. At that time the foal is freeze branded and the foal's own DNA is put on universal record. When that animal grows up to be a race horse and is entered into a specific race, it is the duty of the paddock judge to check the freeze brand number and ensure the public that they are betting on a specific horse, without question.

Standardbred horses are classified as either *Pacers* or *Trotters* and to describe the difference between the two, is that pacers go forward moving the front and back leg on each side simultaneously, while the trotter is described as diagonally-gaited in that they move the right front and the left hind together at the same time. At races they only race with their own kind and are not mixed as pacers are generally faster than trotters. Not too long ago trainers had to work hard to keep their horse doing its specific gait but nowadays the breeding is so specific and in-depth that the foals pace or trot naturally from birth.

The majority of foals born today in Ontario are as a result of mares having been bred to stallions standing for service in the province and they're eligible for the so-called Ontario Sires Stakes Program. Furthermore, regardless of when the foal is born it is determined to be one year old on the January 1st following its birth. To be more specific if the foal is born on April 21st, 2014 it is determined to be one-year-old on January 1st, 2015 and they become a two-year-old, and three-year-old, or older, each January 1st thereafter. When they become yearlings, on the following March 15th of that year they have to be nominated to race in the Stakes. The payment is made along with the declaration as to whether they are trotters of pacers, and of course their sex as when they first race as two-year-olds they only race in classes with their own sex.

Two-year-olds race approximately only six or seven times and the approximate purse is $20,000 for each start. This money is divided amongst the first five finishers as follows: the winner gets 50%, the horse finishing second gets 25%, third horse gets 12%, fourth gets 8% and finally the fifth and last place gets 5%. The remaining five horses in a ten horse field race for a purse get no remuneration except the experience. It costs roughly $300 to $500 to enter a horse in any given stake race. Usually at the end of the racing season the top 10 money winners in each division then race for the first purse - something in the order of $100,000 and the money is divided as described previously. There are two divisions in the Sires Stakes, the gold and the grassroots, the gold division going for far more money but you are the one to classify them because the gold division goes much faster.

Until last year this Ontario Sires Stakes program was considered the best racing stakes program in the world and many countries and American states copied our program.

Then sometime in mid-2012 the provincial Liberal government announced the cessation of the arrangements that they had made with the different racetracks where casino slots programs had been for the previous 12 years with a percentage of all the slot betting going to horse racing purses, the racetrack itself, and the municipality in which the racetrack was located. It was the government itself that initiated this system, visiting racetracks and suggesting that since Ontario was going to go into the casino slot betting system that they would like to use the racetracks as the physical location of the actual casinos, thereby preventing them from spending money in this area when at the same time they would be helping the horse racing industry. Of every dollar wagered in the slot machines 10% went to the racetrack, 10% to the horsemen's purses and 5% to the resident municipality. The other 75% went directly to the government of Ontario.

As I said before that had been the practice for 12 years until the decision to change brought about a disaster in the horse racing industry. When this program first started and the purses were increased dramatically many horse owners, including me, immediately spent a lot of money upgrading the quality of their breeding programs so that they would have better horses to race, and obviously make more money. Likewise many top stallions moved from the United States to Canada to be part of this tremendous system which was beneficial to a lot of people, as some 60,000 people in Ontario were directly or indirectly involved in harness racing.

When the government announced that the cessation would take place on March 20, 2013, then the value of horses decreased significantly and many horsemen reduced their involvement in the industry at a considerable financial loss, and a lot of jobs were lost as well. It is also a fact that many of the grooms, who actually provided the every-day care of the horses and who were born into the industry and had little formal education, many between 40 and 60 years of age, are now finding it difficult to find employment and will become a burden on the said government of Ontario.

CHAPTER 10 - POLITICS

From my time as a very young boy, I clearly remember hearing my father speak on political issues on an almost daily basis, and I guess that from being in that environment I too took an interest in politics. The best way I can describe that feeling is that when you hear of some controversial subject anywhere in the area or even the world your mind sort of drifts to how you personally would solve the problem, if you were in a position to do so. With that sort of mentality I knew that someday I would probably become involved at some political level.

In 1987, about the time that I was ending my career of managing the Rideau Carleton Raceway, there was an election coming up in Ontario and, since I was raised in a liberal environment, I decided to *throw my hat into the ring* as a possible candidate. At a subsequent nomination meeting to elect a Liberal candidate, another person and myself ran as potential candidates.

Without going into all the details I was elected to represent the Liberal Party in Carleton County for a seat at Queens Park in Toronto. The riding had a lifelong history of being a Conservative stronghold, never once having elected a Liberal standard-bearer to represent the County. Incidentally, my father had run as a Liberal candidate in 1943 against Holly Acres – I distinctly remember being somewhere in England as a Canadian soldier and having the privilege of voting in our various ridings back home and voting for my dad. He was defeated by some 7000 votes, typical of the history of politics in Carleton County, always voting strongly Conservative since the time of Sir John A. McDonald, Canada's first Prime Minister.

I had the advantage, however, of having the name *Armitage* which at least had not had any family member in jail, but rather my dad and two uncles having served in their respective townships as councillors or reeves, and as Wardens of the County on different occasions. My Uncle Jim had for years been a Justice of the Peace.

Deviating a bit here, I recall as a boy being at my bachelor uncle's home when two men came to have him rule on a dispute between them. My uncle, the Justice, had each of them put five dollars on the table and then instructed one of the men to be totally quiet while the other gave his side of the story. Then when he had completed his version of the dispute he was told to be quiet while the other man related his side, after which my uncle spoke at length giving his decision on the matter, had them shake hands and he bid them adieu. It seems to me now, in retrospect, that things were settled better in those days than today's rather lengthy and expensive court cases.

At the outset of my own campaign for election I felt that I was reasonably well known having been a veterinarian in the area for years, so I decided that since I was up against a strong and established Conservative population and a twenty-year-tried-and-confident candidate that, where possible, I would make it known that I was running as Roly Armitage and not necessarily as a Liberal candidate and that I personally would like to have the privilege of showing the people in Carleton County that I would bring them recognition in Toronto. In the past they had really been neglected, always being taken for granted because it was not necessary for the province to do anything for the riding knowing their conservative candidate was a *shoe-in*. The party would therefore spend their election budget on vote-catching improvements in areas where they had a battle.

After my decision to proceed I appointed a financial officer to collect money to cover my election expenses. I had signs made using the colours green and white more or less as an environmental touch, and to get away from the true Liberal red. As I stated, my effort was to be elected as Roly Armitage and not necessarily the Liberal candidate. I might add at this point that the financial response was fantastic as many people came forward with cheques, a good indication that I personally was on the right path.

When the official word GO was given to start campaigning and with my appointed candidate chairman in place, we set out to cover the area involved which extended all the way from Arnprior in the west to Manotick in the east, a distance of 50 or 60 miles. Meetings were held asking for volunteers in given areas to campaign with me going door-to-door. The longer I was in the campaign the more confident I was that I had a chance to be elected. When we started the campaign my body weight was 250 pounds and when we finished some 30 days later my weight was 225. I remember distinctly that instead of walking I ran from door-to-door and many of my volunteers were a bit frustrated but nevertheless proud of my effort to cover more ground. I might add that at each and every door I introduced myself as Roly Armitage, a candidate in the upcoming election, and unless I was specifically asked what party I represented I didn't mention the word Liberal. I wanted my name to be familiar as it would be on the ballot form on election day.

I must say that the whole campaign ran very smoothly with the exception of one specific area where I, along with the Conservative and NDP candidates, was asked to be at a specific location to answer questions regarding a new Hydro line that was being constructed running through Kanata, crossing Eagleson Road and directly running over a public school.

Some time before this meeting a woman had parked her baby carriage, with a child in it, in front of the bulldozers directing them to discontinue with the line that would cross over the school stating that the electrical rays generated from the lines were dangerous to human health, and particularly growing children.

At the meeting this same woman asked each candidate what we were going to do about it, starting first with the Conservative candidate who said he was deeply concerned and would direct the route of the line to turn right and proceed down the Hope Side Road. The NDP candidate reiterated his response but I was a novice to questions such as this, where you tell people what they want to hear rather than what you believe to be the right course of action. In my case I told her that these rays were generally thought not to be a problem and to authenticate this I explained that there is a virtual cobweb of wires over both Toronto and Ottawa which have caused no undue health problems; further the planned route of the line had already been authorized by the city of Ottawa and properties purchased to build the structures needed to support the lines. I said that to run the line down the Hope Side Road would be out of the question as it would take years for the hydro to purchase the lands needed to do this.

This woman sent a pamphlet to every home in Bridlewood, some one thousand homes in all, stating that I personally had no concerns for the health and welfare of children and to make sure I was not elected. Since it was near the end of the campaign I had no time to counteract her statement and so suffered the consequences. I might add that

I won the city of Kanata in general by 9000 votes to my opposition's total of 7000 but was defeated soundly in the Bridlewood section of Kanata where a potential 1000 votes or more existed. In retrospect this was the reason for my defeat as a potential member of provincial Parliament in Queens Park.

When the final account was tallied on election night I was declared the winner by the radio stations in their early predictions according to the numbers in at that time, but as the final count was established I had been defeated by the Conservative with a total of 15,700 for him and 15,350 for me, with the NDP far back.

I lost the election because I told the lady with the baby carriage the facts and the truth, and obviously that is not always the way to proceed if you want to get elected. I might however, state that I won every poll in West Carleton where everybody knew me.

• • •

In 1989, following my ten years as president and general manager of Rideau Carleton Raceway, I resumed my veterinary practice. One day in September of the next year I was at the Carp Fair and as I was leaving I met Jack Shaw who had been my campaign manager during my run for provincial election in 1987. He asked me if I would consider running for mayor of West Carleton. My reply to Jack was, "Jack I don't even know where the town hall is." His immediate reply was, "I will show you if you would consider running." I told him that I would get back to him. The election was not till November so I had lots of time to think about it.

I found that the Township office was on the Carp Road near the airport and the property, which previously had been with the Department of Agriculture, was rented from the federal government. In due course I made a decision to run for the office of Mayor and went to the office to determine how and where applications were made.

I remember the clerk, in a turtleneck sweater sitting at a desk, chewing gum. I informed him that I wished to make an application for council and, not rising, he pointed to a pile of application forms over on a table and told me I needed to fill one out and return it to him. After reading the instructions which called for ten property owners to sign my application I left the building. Returning to Carp, I went to the restaurant of Ernie and Laurie where there was a gathering of patrons having coffee. One person was John Caldwell and I presented the form for signature to him which he, knowing me well, immediately signed and then passed it around for further endorsements. Before I left the establishment I had my ten signatures and returned to the Township office with my application form which I presented to the clerk who was still sitting there chewing gum.

I presented the document to him, which obviously indicated I was running for mayor and could possibly, in the future, be his boss. Nevertheless he stayed seated and pointed me to a book on another stand which contained information regarding the rules and regulations pertaining to the election.

When I walked out of the office, I thought if I ever got elected there would have to be new instructions for that clerk regarding the respect and manners extended to the taxpayers or visitors as I deemed the Clerk's office to be the centre of activity for the township.

There was one other candidate for mayor, a former head of council. He was an absolute gentleman throughout the campaign during which time I visited every home in West Carleton and eventually I was declared the winner two to one. During one of the all-candidates meetings my opponent said that I personally was only running in the office as a stepping stone to be a candidate for the upcoming federal election the next year. I assured him that was not the case and that if I was elected I would fulfill my term.

In retrospect I was sorry that I had made that statement. At that time I never thought that I might run for federal politics in the upcoming federal election in 1993. However, when the election was called I was visited by a very important individual who asked me if I would consider running for Liberal office and told that if elected I would be offered the ministerial position of Minister of Veterans Affairs in the cabinet of Jean Chretien. A short time later Ian Murray, who was considering making an application to run in our riding, came to me and asked me if I was considering running because he didn't feel he could beat me in a nomination and even said he would support me if I ran. The chances of election of a Liberal in the county was fairly obvious by that time, and I seriously considered jumping ship - I rued the declaration that I had made to the other mayoral candidate when I said that if elected I would finish my term as mayor.

The Mayor

That I did, and went on to complete my four years as mayor. I think one of the greatest accomplishments was getting sewer and water for the entire village of Carp because prior to that in the downtown section wells were contaminated and, believe it or not, there was still some outdoor toilets in the village. I remember one day while sitting in my office my secretary handed me my mail and there was this one important piece that came from the Premier of Ontario stating that they were stressing the installation of sewer and water in any village that was in possession of engineering drawings but were unable to proceed with the installation because of lack of funds. I spoke immediately with our township engineer who informed me that the drawings were available so I called Toronto and made arrangements for a meeting the next day.

Doug Rivington, our engineer, and I met the people involved at the appointed hour, and the rest is history as we were approved. Meetings were held with the city of Ottawa, the provincial government and ourselves, to determine the cost and the appropriate percentages which would be levied to each party. It was agreed that the province pay 75%, the city 15%, and the homeowners 10% based on per square-foot lot frontage.

The only real problem was the fact that all wells had to be sealed and that everyone had to use communal water along with the sewage system. One gentleman gathered more than 100 homeowners on the higher elevated areas of the village and came to a Council meeting demanding that we leave their uncontaminated wells alone. Since it was established that the wells had to be sealed to proceed with the whole contract, myself, with the backing of the entire Council informed the group that this could not be the case, that the contracts had been let and that we were going to proceed.

After they continued to come to the microphone one by one to say their bit, I stated that we had other things to proceed with this evening and that only two more speakers would be allowed. After these two people had spoken in defiance of our decision, the leader of the group got up to speak and I immediately objected and said no, the two additional people have spoken already so no one else is being heard. He immediately pointed his finger at me and stated emphatically, "Mr. Mayor you will pay for this decision." And that I did. In an upcoming election against Betty Hill for a seat on regional government I was defeated by only 15 votes, and in retrospect his prediction came true since Mrs. Hill got more than 100 votes in Carp.

He was right in declaring that I would *pay* for the council's decision at that meeting of the village council but I am proud that the value of properties jumped immediately in Carp. Later I was told that the gentleman who had done all the complaining got a handsome price for his property when he sold and left town.

• • •

Nearing the termination of my time as mayor, a decision to close the Diefenbunker was made by the federal government and more particularly the military due to the termination of the so-called Cold War. Many people came forward with ideas as to what to do with the project. Some wanted to fill it with sand and forget about it; others had ideas for its use, one being a place to manufacture fireworks. I suggested that it had real public interest and that it should be turned over to West Carleton Township for a dollar until a decision could be made about its future. Council was against this as the cost of keeping it open for any use would be too costly, let alone profitable.

The radio system in the bunker was still in wraps and had never been used. A reporter from CBC and I got it running one day and we made a public newscast on CBC from the site and then closed it back down. The military, in spite of several requests by forward-thinking citizens, such as Dr. Barry Bruce and Dr. Bob Borden, to leave it intact for possible museum purposes, proceeded to remove every item from the building. Without going into any details, everyone knows that much of the material that had been removed was brought back to the bunker and was turned over to a very effective local committee to establish the museum that it is today, one of the most successful museums in Canada for tourist attraction and attendance.

• • •

In 1991, a year after I'd been elected mayor we were informed by the federal Department of Agriculture that they required the offices in which we were established for their own use and we were given one year to vacate. We looked at several places where the township offices could move but nothing was suitable. Since previous councils had wisely set money aside for establishment of a permanent site and construction of their own building, the whole Council decided to proceed with the endeavour. We asked the public for proposed sites that could be purchased and many were brought forth.

As a group we visited the many sites and finally decided on two as favourites. One being on the corner of the Carp Road and the Kinburn Side Road, the other being in the village of Carp. A public council meeting was held in the Kinburn Community Center and several people attended for a full discussion on the two sites and public input was invited. Finally the full council voted on the proposed site, with myself in the chair. Since we had six councillors they were to vote and if there was a tie, then I would make the final decision. Brown, MacMillan, Rietzma and Eastman voted for the Carp Road-Kinburn Side Road site while Caldwell and Kemp voted for the Carp site. Since the vote was four to two no vote by me was necessary, but when summing up the meeting I publicly stated that had I been called on to vote that I preferred the Carp site, to let everybody know where I stood.

My concern was not necessarily the Carp Road-Kinburn Side Road site itself, but the water quality in that area was bad. A decision was made that night that if the water quality was bad when a drill was completed on site then the move to Carp would be the final choice. Drilling was done by Stanton and the first well was absolutely unsuitable; however they said that if they drilled on the edge of the property closer to the Kinburn Side Road then there was a chance of getting good water. Consequently a second well was drilled and since it was found to be satisfactory, the building, which had been designed by Barry Hobin and Associates and accepted by Council, was approved and built by the Thomas Fuller Construction Company.

Dr. Roland Armitage Hall located in the West Carleton Municipal Building

CHAPTER 11 - CARP AIRPORT

After my period on Council I spent two years on industrial development of the Carp Road which my predictions then and still are, that this corridor between Stittsville and Carp will develop into a major road like Woodroffe Avenue with City water supplied to everyone including Carp village including a developed Carp airport where people living there will have their own planes and cars in separate buildings beside their houses. The Carp airport was owned by the city and in a terrible state of repair, even though the manager Bob Bordon and his son were doing a noble job with no support and low pay in keeping it even half viable.

Since I had been on city Council and pretty well knew the workings of each and every department and the people involved including the mayor, financial controller, councillors and staff, they came to me and asked if I would consider taking over the management of the airport. Remuneration and my job description were established after several meetings and I took over the job.

There was very little available equipment or wherewithal on-site so I negotiated with the city to get whatever equipment I needed from their surplus departments, and funds to get the necessary work done, such as grass cutting, road maintenance, and snow removal. There was an urgent need for housing for private aircraft with many parked outside and subject to weather conditions. I called a number of pilots together with the suggestion that I would build a communal hangar to support as many as 20 aircraft, with each individual having their own separate stall and entrance. I entered into discussions on the construction of this building with Bruce Baird of Baird Construction, who was a pilot himself. We discussed the estimated cost and then I got back to the interested pilots and informed them of the description of the proposed project and that I needed a $10,000 down payment before construction, with the remainder to be paid immediately upon being presented with a key to the door. The response was very enthusiastic and the project was a *go on green.*

The city had agreed to back my loan at the bank and the venture was so successful that there was an immediate demand for second 20-stall hangars which were also built and filled. Shortly thereafter the demand was yet evident for construction of a third such hangar but was put on hold because the city had been approached by a John Phillips from the United States who had a group interested in purchasing the airport lands of two hundred acres, but not including the area associated with the airport proper which would remain a separate entity. They would rent it for their purposes as it was their intent to build homes with adjoining carports and airplane hangars.

Since the actual development had to be put on hold until there was an actual sale and the necessary permits to bring the proposed scheme to fruition, my duties were relegated to the management of the airport itself where taxes were levied by the city upon the individual hangars, and other tenants such as First Air, Helicopters Canada, and a private pilot training school. The total costs of running the airport were then at a break-even point and the city was happy to be off the hook in financing the operation.

Up to this point it was the policy of the airport that anyone owning a building there only owned the structure but not the land upon which it sat. Then a new problem arose. Luc Pilon, the owner of Helicopter Transport Canada asked me to meet with him and he informed me that he wanted to largely increase his operation but was unwilling to do so unless he could purchase the land to build on.

He told me that he had made a request at the city level to get permission to purchase the land and was refused because of the existing regulations. Some days later I was at breakfast with Bruce Baird and he informed me that Luc Pilon had purchased land at the Arnprior airport, where he intended to move and extend his helicopter base. I was the airport manager at Carp and, thinking about letting this happen to our number one and largest taxpayer was just not something I was going to let happen. I was determined to do something about it. I went immediately to see Luc and said to him, "If I can get you permission to buy the necessary lands to expand within the next five hours will you reverse your decision about going to Arnprior?" To this request he said yes, and I left his office. It took me two hours to contact the city mayor, Bob Chairelli, and I agreed to meet him in Ottawa. I explained to him the gravity of the case and whereby if we lost this tenant, in my opinion, it would be the end of the airport as a viable commodity and that something had to be done. Having been a mayor myself I knew that there was such a thing called the *Mayor's Prerogative* whereby in the case of an emergency, the mayor can act alone and make a decision, such as in this case where there was no time to contact councillors for a reversal of the existing 'no sale of airport lands' condition, if it was in the best interests of the city.

He agreed to think it over and would let me know in an hour. I returned to the Carp airport and awaited his call. I soon received it giving me a positive decision with instructions to inform Luc that arrangements would be made immediately for him to buy and build at Carp. Again, I weigh this as having been one of my major accomplishments during the ten years that I was at the airport.

• • •

I can't let another day go by without mentioning the tremendous help that I had while managing the Carp Airport. When I first came to Carp Airport, Bob Borden and his son were in charge and they also had a man named Ray Kucharik helping part-time. When I took over I could see a lot of good qualities in this man and promoted him to operating manager. I can't remember having seen a man more versatile than he was. He could turn his hand to anything from managing an office to any area of outside work which included being a top-notch mechanic. He came from a hard-working Polish farm family on Calumet Island, Quebec. They were all raised tough, working the farm while dad was in the mines. Assisting him part-time on the airport when needed was a former farmer and private pilot named Neville Johnston who was semi-retired and also a tremendous worker. These men made my job run smoothly as I spent a lot of my airport time with the city, getting things in order.

As I mentioned before John Phillips had purchased the lands on the airport not directly associated with the actual flying areas, like runways and so on, and was to build a terminal building as part of the contract. I must proudly and humbly state that he named it "Roly Armitage Airport Terminal." His aim, along with an assistant engineer, was to plan and build a fly-in community of stand-alone residential homes in one area, as well as homes with attached hangars and car garage. The connecting roads and streets would be built to handle all traffic, with planes having the right of way everywhere. He also planned a communal septic system with water brought in by pipe from the Carp system. At this time in 2014 all permits are in place for a positive go ahead on his plans. However, just recently, Phillips has sold his entire holdings at Carp Airport to a new group of investors but the development is still going on as planned with sufficient financing.

I retired from the airport in 2012 and Kucharik took over as General Manager, but not before I decided to get my flying licence at the ripe old age of 82, which included 40 hours of ground school followed by 18 hours instructional flying lessons. It was determined early that I would never get a license because of my hearing BUT I did fly a Cessna 180 from Carp to Arnprior airport, landed and took off, came back landed again and then took off and flew back to Carp. To this date I have not been close to a small plane again as I am still deaf as a result of my wartime experiences in 1944.

The Terminal

CHAPTER 12 - PERSONAL LIFE

Over the many years that I had been involved in harness racing, I had three sons and, like most children, they just loved to be with the horses. I could see also that it kept them out of mischief, so as soon as possible I got them involved in stall cleaning and general horse care. In each and every case as they got older and into their teens I encouraged them to take jobs during the summer holidays, working with established trainers at various racetracks in the area. This made them feel important because they were making money, and they all learned to be good workers. The only problem with that was, to them, school became secondary in importance and there wasn't much interest in education after grade ten.

Mary and I solved the problem with our eldest son Maxwell (better known as Mick) by sending him off to boarding school at Ashbury College from where he graduated. He also became deeply involved in music and now has a band, *The Mick Armitage Band*, which he has been operating for the past 30 years, as well as working as a contractor for CGI (*Consultants to Government and Industry*). He is now at the age when he could draw the old-age pension.

My second son, Blake, after finishing grade 11 worked with me full time on the farm and eventually was made farm manager, where at one point we had a standing stallion for breeding purposes and eight men employed in training horses for other people, including some of our own. We had mares being shipped in to be bred to our stallion and of course they needed to be cared for and fed. At one point there were some 70 animals in our two barns.

Blake, the farmer

Blake, in his off-hours and extra time cut pine logs from the bush and built himself a lovely one-level log home. He married a beautiful local lady named Mary Lou Carrier.

Blake also had an intense interest in fast cars and at one point with another young man, reconditioned a fast Ford product. During the process and before the vehicle's muffler had been installed, he, after having dinner, took the vehicle for a test run late one evening. He felt ill and drove the car back and parked it in the farmyard, shut off the ignition, and lay face down on the seat. He vomited while lying there and aspirated it into his lungs. He died in that very vehicle. On the postmortem it was discovered that he had a 20% lethal dose of carbon monoxide in his system which caused his sickness and brought about his death.

I can only say that we were totally and absolutely devastated and at this point the total operation at the farm ceased to exist at such a high level and reverted to just a family-farm affair. This all happened in 1981. I sold the operational part of the

Blake

farm in 1983, which was about half my acreage holdings. Then my wife, Mary, died of cancer in 1985.

After the sale my next son, Donald, and I operated a horse farm on a very limited basis with one hired hand and continued to race horses, but only ones we owned ourselves. Over the next few years we did have some success as Donald became a driver and had reasonable and profitable success. Don won several races for us in the sires stakes and we produced *Armstead Don* who became three-year-old trotter of the year and later we had *Armstead Jim* become a really good winner in excess of $200,000. He was voted aged pacer of the year. Eventually he was sold for $70,000 to be exported to New Zealand as a stallion for breeding purposes.

Donald then retired from working full time in the racing business but continued on a more part time basis. He went to work with the city of Ottawa where he has continued until this date *(2014)* – serving some 30-plus years and is about five years from retirement. Now he is racing his own horse called *Nashville* at Rideau Carleton Raceway and hopes it will make it to the Stake Races on the Ontario circuit.

Emily, Donald, Margaret, and Glenda

I'd like to add that our farm is called *Armstead Farms*, named from the Armitage Homestead, which was one of the founding farms of this area, where my great-great-grandfather who came here in 1836 from Tipperary, South Ireland, settled.

Recently I had a very decent race filly in *Armstead Kyra* who was third best in Ontario in 2012 and repeated again in 2013 being the third best in the Ontario Grass Roots division, earning in excess of $100,000 over the two years. I sold her last year at the Harrisburg sale for $17,000 American dollars. She was by a stallion in Ontario called *Muscle Mass* and I am presently training her full sister, *Armstead Paige*.

Donnie, Roly and Mick at the races

As well as three sons, we also had one daughter, Ann Elizabeth, who was born in 1953 in Quebec. She went to high school there and then went on to the High School of Commerce in Ottawa. She worked in the high-tech industry in Ottawa for many years. She was married to Wayne Shepherd, a fine young man from Renfrew who was a graduate electrician. Unfortunately Wayne became affected with ALS, often referred to as Lou Gehrig disease, and even though much research has been done, it is always terminal. Wayne died a very young man and Ann continued on at work in Kanata. I might add that Ann was very much her mother's girl and stayed away from the stable and horses.

Speaking of her mother (nee Mary Spearman from Stittsville, Ontario, as I mentioned before in my writings) - she and I were married June 28, 1947 two years after I came home from overseas. When I was over there she wrote me twice a week for almost four years.

God could never have found a better wife for me as she supported me financially, working all the time as a bookkeeper while I attended University in Guelph and then was front and centre mixing veterinary drugs for my practice, attending the phone - making and receiving calls - with farmers, running the office both manually and figuratively, mailing and collecting the bills and, most important, she was steadfast in raising our four children as I was on the road most of the time. Even with all those responsibilities she was an immaculate housekeeper and a true homemaker in every sense of the word.

We were very happy in our marriage and had a few lengthy vacations. Alas, Mary contracted Multiple Myeloma, a form of bone cancer which is untreatable and after four painful years she died a young woman at 60 years of age on March 15, 1985, just after we had built a smaller home and were looking forward to all the plans we had for the future. One being that we would attend the celebrations in Holland for the 50th anniversary of the end of the war, where I wanted to show her all the nice parts and places that I had told her about over the years.

• • •

Time marches on, and I remarried in January of 1990. I was most fortunate in meeting a rather beautiful young lady some 24 years my junior in Karen Flahven. She was 41 while I was 65 at the time. I always joked that I got two for the price of one because Karen had a ten-year-old son and he also became part of my life while he went through high school and Algonquin College, graduating as a computer engineer. While he was attending school he had some part time jobs with Nav Canada, an at-arms-length agency of the government in full charge of air traffic in the country. When he graduated they called and offered him part-time work and he must have done a good job because they later took him on permanently. He is now married and they have their own home in Kanata.

Karen and I were very happily married and travelled extensively until she became sick with a liver problem. We made trips to the Toronto General Hospital where she had been directed to be examined regarding the possibilities of a liver transplant. After several trips and examinations, blood tests, and so on, she was informed that she was on the list for a transplant and would have to live within an hour's drive of the hospital in the event that a suitable donor liver was available. Of course, we agreed to do this, but it meant some very serious planning on our part.

Karen and myself

Karen was told that one solution was to get a room at a special hotel which gave a very low rate for people awaiting liver transplants. Just as we were about to make arrangements for the move she developed a problem that put her on a *cease transplant* list until things improved.

People are more interested in the facts than the reasons why all these things happen, but the Ottawa doctors in charge of Karen's case said that her body, for whatever reason, was not receptive for a transplant and that was final. Before that Karen was the ultimate believer that she was going to get better after the liver transplant and in anticipation she purchased all the nice things that she was going wear and stored them in appropriate places in our home awaiting that time. Unfortunately that time never came.

Karen had many friends and many knew her belief that there is no life hereafter as she often said, "We come from the earth and we ultimately return to earth." She had one particular friend in horseman John Smith, a very devout Roman Catholic, who said to me one day, "You know what Roly, God is a very forgiving person and knowing Karen as God would, of course, He would see in her the type of person that He admires and she is going to be really surprised. God understands that thinking people might question His authenticity because no one has seen Him but He will take her directly into heaven." After a relatively short period of time it became obvious that Karen's health was steadily declining and the doctors informed me that she was approaching her demise.

She died on July 22nd, 2013 and, according to her wishes, there was no viewing of the body and the funeral was simple with only the family present. Pinecrest Remembrance had her body cremated and I conducted the burial at St Mary's Cemetery on the Ottawa River, with no members of the cloth present. I reiterated the words made by John Smith, and everyone present, including her former husband and son, put earth on her ashes, and we departed.

Karen had said to me that when she died she wanted everyone to come to a party at the so called *Roly Dome* where there would be lots of food, refreshments and my son Mick's band to supply music. Invitations were extended and 300 people attended. 1 must admit that at that moment I was so proud of her, and was honoured by the number of people who came up to me and said so many wonderful things about her.

• • •

I am rather fortunate in having an extended family beyond my own children since I have six grandchildren two of whom are great-grandchildren.

My eldest son Mick has one son Shaun who in turn, with his wife Shannon are the parents of my two great-grandchildren, Blake and Katie, who at this point are eleven and nine respectively and both are above average hockey players. Blake has just returned from a trip to Finland and Sweden as part of a select team sent from the Ottawa District and Katie plays on a boys team.

Four Generations - Donnie, Roly, Mick, Shaun, and Blake, 2013

My son Donald has a daughter Ashley by a previous marriage. She is now married to a farmer in the Trenton area and it is rumoured that she's pregnant and therefore will be presenting me with another great-grandchild. Donald and his present wife Glenda have two girls, Emily is 20 and is studying architectural drafting at Algonquin College and Margaret, 18, is studying to become a nurse, also at Algonquin College.

• • •

Shannon, Katie, Blake, and Shaun

I would like at this time to state a point of interest that my own being here is the result of a man by the name of Benjamin Armitage – nicknamed Big Ben because of his size - coming to Canada in the year 1836 and receiving grants of land on the Ottawa River. Big Ben died one year after his arrival.

Emigrating to Canada with him were his son James and three grandchildren in their teens and early twenties. All boys at one time or another worked in the lumber camps in Western Quebec. One boy, Richard, bought a farm in the Quyon area of Pontiac County and was the beginning of the many Armitages in that area.

Another of the three boys, John, moved to Western Canada and the third boy, Frances David, in 1860 purchased a farm next door to the existing original grant his father had received, married a new young immigrant, Margaret Montgomery, also from Ireland, in 1861, and together built a new log home and raised ten children the youngest being my father Godfrey, born in 1878. So at this point in 2014 my great-grandchild Blake is the eighth direct male line from the beginning *Big Ben* - all incidentally who have planted their feet at one time or another on the very land upon which I now reside, which is Lot 4, Concession 7, in the Township of Torbolton, County of Carleton, now part of the city of Ottawa. This is so because the original owner, my grandfather Francis David, willed it to my dad's brother William James, who in turn willed it to me upon his death in 1952.

The original log house is still on the farm as a storage building and has a registered plaque on the door designating it a heritage building. When the family grew up a new brick house was built on the property and the log home was turned into a deluxe one-horse stable for my Uncle James's horse, Frank. Alas, due to over heated smoke pipes the new brick house was burned down, so my uncle, a bachelor all his life, built a small stable for Frank and evicted him. He renovated the horse's previous quarters back to space for himself and that's where his duties as a Justice of Peace were conducted.

This was his residence until his death at 88 years of age which was the result of an accident that happened by upsetting the coal oil lamp on himself, causing extensive burns. The home had neither electricity nor phone but it was winter and a neighbour who was always on the watch, saw no smoke from his chimney and came to check. He was taken to the hospital and the rest is history.

The original log home of 1860

CHAPTER 13 - A VETERAN NEVER FORGETS

Brother Bill and myself with our medals.

It is amazing that after my discharge from the Army in 1946 and for the next 50 years very little attention was paid by the public in Canada to those who had given their lives in service to the country, or even to veterans in general. However in countries such as the Netherlands and France, they celebrated their freedom yearly with in-depth remembrance. This all changed in Canada when in 1985 the Netherlands opened their homes to Canadian veterans in celebrating their 50th year of freedom from the years of Nazi occupation of their country.

I personally accepted an invitation to a home in Nijmegan through a joint arrangement between Canada and the Netherlands. We, the veterans, only had to register our names with the Canadian authorities stating which city in Holland we wished to be housed in, and they in turn collaborated with the Dutch authorities to contact a family in that area who had indicated their desire to accept a veteran. Then I was informed of the name and address of the family who was going to be my host.

We flew to Amsterdam where buses were standing by to take us to our selected city. When I arrived at a meeting point, which was a golf course outside the city of Nijmegan, we lined up at the reception desk and Dutch people were sitting around in various tables waiting for their appointed veteran. When I gave my name at the desk I was instructed to go forward to table number 12, and sitting there was my host, a woman who, as I remember, welcomed me with a very lengthy hug.

The celebrations that followed during the next few days were most memorable. They were in the city of Apeldoorn where we were treated with the greatest generosity and respect. This loyalty and respect for Canadian veterans by Holland, France, and Belgium has never ended to this date. Just to visit the Canadian cemeteries is an experience to behold as one views the row upon row of gleaming white headstones with the names of young men and women in their late teens and early twenties who gave their all for the freedom we enjoy today.

• • •

Just this past month, on June 10, 2014, I arrived home from having attended the 70th anniversary of the D-Day landings and the following encounters in Normandy and France. I will remember as long as I live the tremendous reception that was extended to Canadian, British, and American veterans.

The Canadian Government arranged for a military aircraft to fly us direct from Ottawa to the Deauville airport in Normandy. I, along with my attendant for the trip, went to the Southway Hotel in Ottawa on the evening of June 2nd where we registered with Veterans Affairs and met the other 76 veterans and their attendants along with a doctor, two nurses, and eleven paramedics who were our caretakers for the trip. We stayed overnight, had breakfast in the morning and then boarded buses that took us to the military base at the Ottawa airport where we boarded a large bus-type aircraft, and we were on our way.

We landed at Deauville airport in France on the morning of June 4th and were immediately bused to a large local racetrack which was our rendezvous area to meet pre-arranged conveyances to our various hotels. In my case a friend from Holland who, along with his sister, had driven down from their home, some eight hours drive, to pick us up and take us to our hotel in Caen, some 25 miles inland.

Lt. Roy Pattinson's grave

Caen, is the city where many of the veterans, if not all of them, would remember many hours and days spent in battle. I personally was wounded, but not too seriously, on the very outskirts of Caen, and my own officer Lt. Roy Pattinson was killed on July 29th, 1944. He was buried in Beny sur Mer Cemetery just a few miles inland from Courcelles sur Mer where we landed – it was then called Juno Beach. While we were in the Juno Beach area our buses took us down to the actual beach where some of us collected an empty water bottle of sand to take home and then went to the cemetery at Beny sur Mer close by. Needless to say I visited Lt. Pattinson's grave and paid him homage along with others who had been comrades back then.

The whole event was very memorable and nostalgic for many of us veterans who unanimously agreed that things were far more pleasant here now than 70 years ago.

My friends from Holland stayed with us that day, had dinner that evening and then they went on their separate ways for the event because, as far as we were concerned, the total event was regimented and planned. All roads near the Juno Beach area were closed to public traffic so there was no way that they could participate further with us for the final June 5th and 6th celebrations. There were some 14 nations involved, along with many dignitaries from each country including Queen Elizabeth, Prince Philip, Prime Minister Stephen Harper, Hon. Julian Fantino, our Veterans Affairs Minister, and surprisingly, Mr. Putin from Russia.

Shaking hands with Prime Minister Stephen Harper

While in Caen, the hospitality extended to the veterans was fantastic. I recall one evening at the hotel, I had just arrived from a rather active and tiring day and flopped into a big armchair with an air of relief and, since the bar was in my view, I signalled to the bartender and made the statement, "Garçon, how good is your elbow? I would like a double shot of cognac, specifically Remi Martin." With that the waiter said "Bon, pour vous." and at the same moment a loud endorsement came from a French patron at the bar stating, "And the bill is on me." This was the type of respect and welcome that was extended to us.

Another example: we were waiting for a taxi at a designated area where in France there are areas marked TAXI on certain street corners where if you desire a taxi, you just stand there, and if a taxi is driving by and for hire they pull up and you pop in. On two occasions while we were standing there with medals on, obviously identifying us as veterans, I had a normal citizen drive up, stop and say, "Jump in, where can I take you?"

In Caen itself my memory of when we were there during the war was that the city was in ruins as a result of the bombings and shellings. To view it today was such a tremendous contrast, everything having been restored. It reminds you of when we often look at something such as a building or any object in bad repair, that it is just questionable whether you should repair it or take it down and start all over again. I said to my attendant, "Connie, one place I have to see is St. Peter's Cathedral where on one particular night I had taken refuge with a whole lot of other soldiers because it was raining cats and dogs." We went there and I showed her the very spot were I slept the night away. She took a picture of me at the front door. Also not far up the Orne River, just on the outskirts of the city, is where I got my only injury during the war.

Speaking again about the tremendous hospitality extended to us I want to say also that my assistant and I stayed the last two days of our trip with a French family, M.

and Mme Jean Coutey in their beautiful and cosy home, just a few miles from Juno Beach along with their three sons. Two sons are now in university and the youngest is in his last year of high school.

My late wife Karen and I had stayed with them ten years previously. At that time the French people had advertised their homes to house Canadian veterans returning to revisit Juno beach. I recall that they stated in their advertisement that whoever came to their home had to like children. Of course we accepted and had a very memorable stay. It was amazing seeing the boys again after ten years all grown up. I count the Couteys among my very close friends. In particular, Jean has been studying the history of World War 11 in depth.

On our flights both to and from France the plane had to fly at 12,000 feet altitude, rather than 30,000, so that the air we were flying through was more oxygenated making it easier for those veterans with breathing problems to enjoy the flight. Since the air at this level is much more dense, it was necessary for the airplane to land at Gander airport on both flights to replace the fuel that the aircraft used in flying at that level.

The Prime Minister's wife, Laureen, flew over with us and offered us as a treat some chocolate chip cookies baked in their home on Sussex drive, but she smiled and said, "However I will admit that I personally was not the chef."

Hon. Julian Fantino, Canada's Veterans Affairs Minister was on the flight with us and stated that he thought he could make the same trip possible to Amsterdam next year, to celebrate the 70th anniversary of the end of WW2 and the liberation of Holland.

I might add that the return was uneventful and I am thankful to the Government of Canada for making this expense-free trip possible for the veterans and their personal attendants. Of interest, the youngest veteran on this trip was 89 and the oldest was 101 which means they were 19 to 31 years of age back then.

• • •

Even though all of us veterans are in our twilight years, the memories of our wartime experiences remain indelibly imprinted on our minds. Each day during that time we were aware that it might be our last and thus our consciousness was more acutely attuned to how precarious and precious life is.

I was recently notified that the Government of France was awarding me the Legion of Honour Medal. When I was informed of this I felt very humbled because my mind was immediately transported back to those times, and my comrades who never got the opportunity to experience all the richness that life has to offer. They lie where they fell in battle; forever young but with their full potential unrealized.

CHAPTER 14 - EPILOGUE

I can't end the writings in this book without discussing the problems of growing old. I have named the book *The Way It Was and Now*. I can emphatically state without question that, except for the sad times of losing friends during the war and since, and more specifically, when I lost my wives and son, I have enjoyed every step of the way recounted in *The Way it Was*.

But I can also just as emphatically state that I'm not all that taken up with the *Now* part and its inevitable feelings of growing old.

My mind goes back to when I was a boy and, like every other young lad there was no end to my energy - I could go night and day without an ache or a pain. Even in my later years I always exercised extensively and participated in as many sports as possible, not being any good any of them except maybe an above average hockey player.

Almost every day of my life the first thing I did in the morning, regardless of whether I was at home or away in some other city on business, was to get up and go for a mile run. I can't say that I did this all the time when I was in active and busy every-day veterinary practice, but on any slack day I made sure that I did the run.

I can recall that on my 60th and 70th birthdays I ran around the concession roads here at my home, a distance of six miles, and on my 80th birthday I ran the first three miles and was disappointed that I had to walk the last three, the first indication that age was catching up with me.

Now that I am nigh on 90 years of age I can also emphatically state that I'm not near the man I used to be and have a hell of a time walking let alone running 1000 feet. I have extensive arthritis in my back and Post-Shingles Neurotic pain on the left side of my waist but aside from that I just passed a rather extensive medical exam so that I could participate in the return to Normandy for the 70th Anniversary of D Day landings and ensuing battles in Caen and Falaise. And I am eagerly looking forward to going again in May of 2015, to Holland for the celebrations of the cessation of WW2 and the Canadian participation in bringing about their liberation from the Nazi occupation.

Oh! Excuse me, I just heard my knee crack when I swiveled in my computer chair where I have spent many hours working on my book *The Way it Was and Now.*

The Way it Was and Now

ADDENDUM

Over my lifetime I have had the good fortune to receive many awards and honours. Each time this happened I felt very honoured but also humbled, because I knew there were many others who were equally or more deserving and did not receive such recognition.

To not include mention of those honours might give the erroneous impression that they are not appreciated or valued. Nothing could be further from the truth.

It is for that reason I have decided to list them here.

1961   Citizen of the Year, Shawville

1974-76   President of Canadian Standardbred Horse Society

1976-80   President of Canadian Trotting Association

1982   Veterinarian of the Year - Ontario Veterinarians Association

1999   Canadian Horse Racing Hall of Fame

2000   Ottawa Sports Hall of Fame

2000   Queen's Jubilee Medal

2006   Key to the City of Ottawa

2007   Roly Armitage Airport Terminal Building - Carp

2011   Dr. Roland Armitage Hall in West Carleton - City of Ottawa

2013   Ontario Veterinary College, University of Guelph Distinguished Alumni of the Year

Military Medals

France and Germany Star, 1939-45 Star (6 months or more in action)

Defence of Britain (in England one year before D Day)

Victory Medal WW2

Canadian Volunteer Medal

Normandy Defence Medal

National Order of the Legion of Honour – Government of France, 2014

THE LAST WORD

Although I have known Roly Armitage for many years it is only while working with him during these past months that I have come to appreciate his depth of character. He is a man of intelligence, honesty and integrity who has lived life to the fullest and always on his own terms, not allowing temporary setbacks to discourage him from continuing to pursue his goals. Those goals have usually been to make things better for a specific group or the community at large.

Never during our many hours of conversations have I heard him make a mean-spirited comment about anyone or any group of people. His respect for others has nothing to do with their race, religious beliefs, sexual orientation, education or economic status. Such tolerance and understanding is extremely rare in people of his generation and is the mark of an outstanding human being. I believe that it is this generosity of spirit that has been the foundation upon which all his accomplishments have been built.

During the creation of this book he did his part - the writing - allowing me free rein to do the formatting, designing and editing without being hindered by a micromanaging author. It has been a very enjoyable process.

In all sincerity,

Mary Watson Montague

39641224R00097

Made in the USA
Charleston, SC
17 March 2015